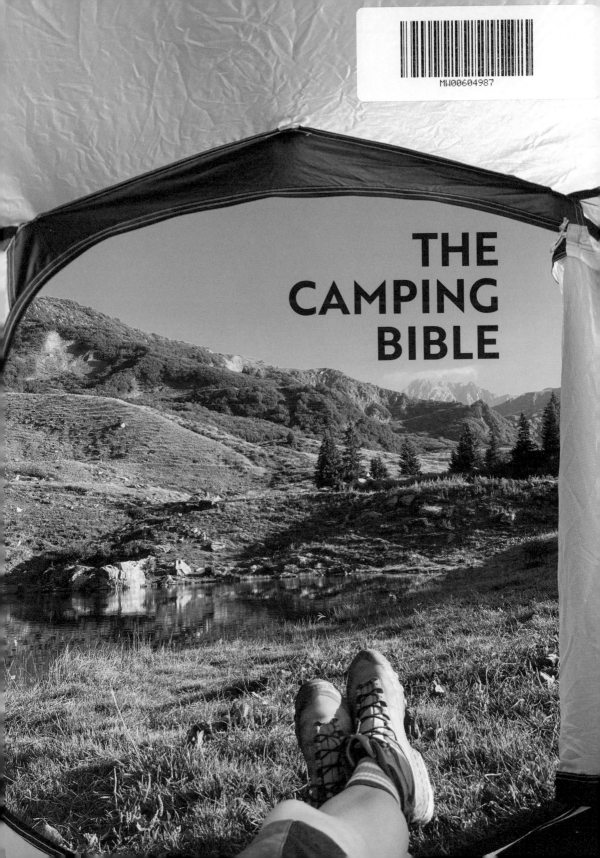

THE
CAMPING
BIBLE

MW00604987

CONWAY
Bloomsbury Publishing Plc
50 Bedford Square, London, WC1B 3DP, UK
29 Earlsfort Terrace, Dublin 2, Ireland

BLOOMSBURY, CONWAY and the Conway logo
are trademarks of Bloomsbury Publishing Plc

First published in Great Britain 2024

Copyright © Jen & Sim Benson, 2023
Illustrations © Alister Savage and Dave Saunders, 2023
Photographs © Jen & Sim Benson, except where stated
otherwise on page 288

Jen & Sim Benson have asserted their right under
the Copyright, Designs and Patents Act, 1988, to be
identified as Authors of this work

For legal purposes the Acknowledgements on page 288
constitute an extension of this copyright page

All rights reserved. No part of this publication may be
reproduced or transmitted in any form or by any means,
electronic or mechanical, including photocopying,
recording, or any information storage or retrieval system,
without prior permission in writing from the publishers

This book is a guide for when you spend time outdoors.
Undertaking any activity outdoors carries with it some
risks that cannot be entirely eliminated. For example,
you might get lost on a route or caught in bad weather.
Before you spend time outdoors, we therefore advise
that you always take the necessary precautions, such as
checking weather forecasts and ensuring that you have
all the equipment you need. Any walking routes that are
described in this book should not be relied upon as a sole
means of navigation, so we recommend that you refer to
an Ordnance Survey map or authoritative equivalent.

This book may also reference businesses and venues.
Whilst every effort is made by the author and the publisher
to ensure the accuracy of the business and venue
information contained in our books before they go to
print, changes to such information can occur during the
production and lifetime of a publication. Therefore, we also
advise that you check with businesses or venues for the
latest information before setting out.

All internet addresses given in this book were correct
at the time of going to press. Bloomsbury Publishing Plc
does not have any control over, or responsibility for, any
third-party websites referred to or in this book. The author
and the publisher regret any inconvenience caused if some
facts have changed or sites have ceased to exist, but can
accept no responsibility for any such changes.

A catalogue record for this book is available from
the British Library

Library of Congress Cataloguing-in-Publication
data has been applied for

ISBN: PB: 978-1-8448-6628-1;
ePub: 978-1-8448-6627-4;
ePDF: 978-1-8448-6629-8

10 9 8 7 6 5 4 3 2 1

Typeset in Aestetico and designed by Austin Taylor
Printed and bound in China by Toppan Leefung Printing

FSC
www.fsc.org

MIX
Paper | Supporting
responsible forestry
FSC® C104723

To find out more about our authors and
books visit www.bloomsbury.com and
sign up for our newsletters

Jen and Sim Benson

THE CAMPING BIBLE

THE COMPLETE GUIDE TO LIFE UNDER CANVAS

CONWAY

LONDON · OXFORD · NEW YORK · NEW DELHI · SYDNEY

CONTENTS

Introduction

Camping holds a special place in our hearts, as well as in our lives. We both grew up doing it. From sleepovers in friends' gardens to annual camping trips to Norfolk, Wales, the Lake District and France, sleeping under canvas was something we were both accustomed to by an early age, and that quickly became a part of who we are.

In our late teens, craving bigger, wilder adventures, it was camping we turned to. Separately, we took our tents to Ireland, Iceland and the Himalayas. In our twenties, after we met while funding our university studies working in an outdoor shop, camping became our together time, our home for weekends of rock climbing, running and adventure racing.

When we became parents, camping remained just as important as ever, and the size of our tent has gradually grown with our family. A decade ago, camping changed our lives entirely. Craving more time together, more adventures, greater opportunities to write and fewer bills, we moved out of our rented house, swapped our sensible family car for a pick-up truck, and lived in a tent for a year, exploring Britain's wild places. At the time, our daughter was three and our son just six months old, which might sound like a challenge too far. But that year under canvas – which in the end became 18 months – changed everything for us,

and all of it for the better.

These days, while we're happy to have four solid walls and a roof to call home, camping remains something that, for us, is deeply connected with choice, freedom, wildness, simplicity and even a bit of rebellion. We're always on the lookout for those special places where all four of us, along with the dog, can have amazing adventures that suit our varying likes and abilities. Places where we can focus on the important things: spending time together, surrounded by the sounds, sights and smells of nature, and embracing fun, freedom and the chance to learn about and experience somewhere new, all in a way that's affordable.

We often talk about our adventure under canvas, sharing our memories of that time. Refusing to conform to the expected, accepted course of life, we once did something different, and every camping trip reconnects us with that feeling. While living in a tent for 18 months with two kids under four might not be something everyone wants to do, that sense of freedom, autonomy and self-sufficiency that even a short camping trip brings is one we think everyone should experience on a regular basis. This book is a guide to that end.

▶ Hammocks work brilliantly for relaxing as well as sleeping. Our Ticket to the Moon (TTTM) Pro hammock gets more use in the day than at night

The art of living outdoors

For us, the art of camping lies in living simply, well. It's about paring back our busy, hyperconnected modern lives and embracing the many joys of living more slowly, connecting more meaningfully, paying better care and attention to each and every moment. In everyday life, rushing through our daily rituals as quickly and efficiently as possible in order to get on to the next thing leaves little time in which to properly savour them. From waking up and making the first coffee of the day to cooking and eating together, some of the most important things we do become barely noticeable as they whizz past in a frenzy of activity. But when we're camping, these small yet significant moments turn out to be those that bring us the greatest joy and satisfaction.

Camping's more laid-back pace opens up time and space to allow us to fully appreciate the simpler things in life: fetching water, getting the stove burning well, hand-grinding coffee beans, listening to the percolator bubble and watching the fragrant steam rising into the fresh morning air… And then the coffee … sipped slowly, warming hands and reviving minds over an easy conversation about what adventures the day ahead might hold. Of course, it tastes a thousand times better, too.

▼ Making the most of the stellar views at Dark Skies Camping, Cambrian Mountains, Wales

▶ Primus Lite+

Sleeping under canvas puts us at the very heart of a place, lying with an ear to the earth; appreciating the natural rhythms of day and night, darkness and light; tuning into the sights, sounds and scents of the natural world. With the insulation of houses, cars, even campervans and caravans stripped away, camping puts us centre stage as nature's drama unfolds all around. It's this lack of solid walls and doors that makes camping a great way to connect with others – campsites are often sociable places where the kids can run in free-range herds while the grown-ups swap stories over a beer or two. When home is a few sheets of colourful fabric and everything from space and washrooms to mealtime conversations is shared, it's hard not to feel part of one big, dynamic community.

Done well, camping can also be a sustainable and low-impact means of getting away, at a budget that suits everyone. Demanding little in the way of resources after the initial outlay on equipment, living under canvas can be rewarding and enjoyable all year round as long as you have the right kit and know how to use it – and there's plenty more on that later on in this book.

Camping and well-being

There's some fascinating, although not unsurprising, research showing the numerous benefits to our mental and physical health to be derived from spending time outdoors, surrounded by nature, particularly if we're being active at the same time. Connection with nature has been found to help with mental health problems such as anxiety and mild to moderate depression, with the greatest effects resulting from combining being outdoors with physical activity. Even simply having a view of nature boosts working memory and other aspects of cognitive function.

Camping has its own set of benefits, aside from those of simply being outdoors.

A major study published in 2022, The Outjoyment Report, was commissioned by The Camping and Caravanning Club and undertaken by a team of academics at Sheffield Hallam University and Liverpool John Moores University (LJMU).

The study surveyed nearly 11,000 people, finding that regular campers reported higher levels of happiness, connectedness to nature, well-being and flourishing compared with non-campers. Campers also reported lower stress levels than non-campers and were more likely to be active in the outdoors, taking part in a range of activities including walking, cycling and bird-watching. An incredible 97 per cent of campers cited happiness as their top motivator for going camping – time under canvas is clearly very good for us.

Other research suggests that coastal locations provide the most restorative experience to campers, with forests and mountains a joint second, while urban parks offer the least restoration – findings that are well worth taking into account when planning your own trips.

▶ Bikepacking in the Brecon Beacons

The essential ingredients of an amazing camping trip

One of the most brilliant things about camping is that it is almost endlessly customisable, enabling adventures of a magnitude and variety to suit everyone. Tents come in a vast array of designs and purposes, allowing you to live and sleep wherever you choose to pitch. Whether it's a fast-and-light backpacking adventure on a long-distance hiking trail, a sea kayak safari exploring remote uninhabited islands, a family camping trip to a sociable campsite, or simply a more regular reconnection with outdoor living and cooking in your garden or other land, camping can do it all.

To get the very best out of any adventure, though, getting your set-up right is really important. From the specifics of clothing and equipment to the craft of setting up camp, and the details of daily life under canvas, sorting the basics will ensure your adventures are as comfortable, safe and life-affirmingly enjoyable as possible.

Throughout this book we'll be exploring all the essentials for great camping trips. We've identified what we think are the key ingredients for every trip, whenever and wherever you choose to go. We'll visit them all in the chapters that follow:

chapter 1	chapter 2	chapter 3	chapter 4	chapter 5	chapter 6
All about tents: suitable for the people, place and conditions.	**Where to camp:** safe, flat, sheltered and in a great place.	**Tent life:** the foundation of successful camping.	**Fire and food:** cooking, food prep and inspiration.	**Adventure time!:** the where and how of amazing camping trips.	**Caring and repairing:** the joy of daily living under canvas.

Camp safety

Camping is generally a safe activity, but there are a few potential risks common to any camping trip, as well as those that are more location-specific. Knowing and understanding these risks helps to prevent accidents and enables everyone to relax and have an enjoyable trip.

Fire and carbon monoxide

Even tents treated with fire-retardant coatings can burn, so if you can possibly avoid it, don't cook or use candles, gas lanterns or gas heaters in a tent. As well as the fire risk, carbon monoxide (CO) poisoning is a real possibility in small, enclosed spaces. If the weather dictates that your cooking needs to be done under cover, make sure the space is well ventilated

▲ With the right kit, even the lightest and most packable set-up – in this case the Nordisk Telemark tent and OMM clothing – can offer warmth and comfort on year-round adventures

and that your stove is near to, but not obstructing, the entrance. It's worth considering taking a carbon monoxide alarm – during our year under canvas, when we used a wood burner in the tent for heat and cooking, we had a CO alarm affixed to a tent pole near to the stove.

When you're setting up your camping space, have a contingency plan in place: being able to exit promptly in the event of a pan fire could save your tent – and even your life. For the same reason, make sure stoves are positioned on a stable, flat surface and out of the way of any main thoroughfare. There's more about cooking and staying warm safely in Chapter 4.

Electricity

Rain and electricity clearly aren't a good mix. When connecting with electric hook-up at a campsite, always use a camping-specific unit, which will have a trip switch and waterproofing.

Pegs and guy lines

Tripping over guy lines and tent pegs is a common cause of camping injuries. Use bright or reflective guy lines or twist LED lights along them, cover the pegs (old tennis balls work well – unless you have a ball-obsessed dog, as we do!), and make sure everyone's aware of the hazards right from the start. Kids running around involved in games tend to forget about mundane things like pegs and are strong candidates for nasty injuries, so it's worth doing all you can to pre-empt and avoid them.

Weather

Check the weather forecast before you leave and, if you can, regularly during your trip. Most tents are designed to handle a bit of bad weather – some better than others – but only if they're pitched well. If there's any chance of less-than-perfect weather, think carefully about where and how you pitch, including the position relative to the wind, potential hazards such as overhead tree branches and flooding, and use all your pegs and guy lines. If strong winds, heavy rain or thunder are predicted, do you still want to go? If so, perhaps consider taking a more robust tent, even if it means sacrificing some living space or adding weight.

If you are camping and hear a thunderstorm approaching, check all guy lines and pegs are secured and tight. Be ready to leave the tent if it sounds like the storm is going to pass close by. A car or the campsite facilities block will be the safest

> Think carefully about where and how you pitch, including the position relative to the wind, potential hazards such as overhead tree branches and flooding.

place to go until the storm has passed. If you're wild camping, seek low ground such as a gully or ditch (be sure it's not somewhere likely to flood) and stay away from trees. This is especially important in a bell tent or tipi with a metal central pole.

Have a plan

If you're staying at a campsite, familiarise yourself with firefighting and first aid equipment before you need it. If you're camping somewhere wilder, a little forward planning helps with avoiding and dealing with risks. Consider what risks are more likely in the environment that you are going into – this could be anything from snake and mosquito bites to hypothermia or sunstroke. Pack emergency kit to deal with anything that is likely, high risk and time dependent. Check out escape routes to somewhere you can get help if needed. Think about how you will summon help: is there phone signal or will you carry a satellite phone or emergency beacon? Where can emergency services get to and how long is it likely to take for help to reach you? If you're somewhere remote, your first aid kit might need to be more comprehensive.

Finally, if you're heading into the wilds, make sure someone knows where you are planning to go and how long you are planning to be. If you haven't contacted them or arrived by a certain time, agree what action they will take, whether that's coming to look for you, alerting the emergency services or both.

Most campsites have drinking water on tap, but if you're wild camping or staying in a country that doesn't have safe tap water you will need to filter, boil or treat your water. The different methods for treating water are explained in Chapter 3.

Insects and other unwelcome guests are best prevented with physical barriers such as clothing and insect nets. Ticks and the diseases they carry are increasingly becoming a problem in wilder areas, in particular damp, grassy, wooded or forested places. Ticks are tiny arachnids of the Ixodida order, with 900 different species present across the world. Because the most common ticks feed on three different hosts during their life cycle, they can transfer blood-borne diseases between animals, including humans. The incidence of diseases such as Lyme disease, for which there is currently no effective vaccine, and tick-borne encephalitis, for which there is an effective vaccine, is increasing and prevention is far better than cure. In tick-prone areas, try to avoid walking through or sitting in vegetation, check yourself regularly so that you can brush ticks off before they bite, or find and quickly remove any that have attached. Check children regularly, especially around the head, neck and ears. If you do find a tick attached, use tick tweezers or a tick card to remove it as soon as possible. Fever or chills after a bite or an expanding bull's-eye rash around the site of the bite all require medical attention.

Larger visitors, such as rats, mice and squirrels, who are usually after an easy snack, are best deterred by good camping practices, thus avoiding attracting them in the first place.

Having an up-to-date knowledge of first aid is a good idea when travelling and camping in wilder areas. We recommend attending a first aid course every few years and carrying a basic first aid kit with you. First aid apps such as the British Red Cross one are a useful resource for dealing with a range of common medical emergencies.

Leave no trace

One of the many great things about camping is the ability to live in and experience nature while leaving no trace when you depart. Once the tent is down and your bags are packed, the site should look exactly as it did when you arrived, other than perhaps a patch of flattened grass. There's a unique joy in living lightly, embracing a temporary, nomadic way of being rather than stamping our presence upon the earth.

When you're camping at a campsite there probably will be evidence of tents pitched before, but you can still aim to leave the pitch in better condition than you found it. We have a bag full of lost pegs we've found on campsites that come in handy when ours bend or break.

Wild camping

The right to wild camp legally is one that is rapidly vanishing as fears of damage, littering and fire increase. For those who have peacefully wild camped for years, with no one any the wiser for it, scenes of litter-strewn, fire-damaged wild camping sites are truly heartbreaking. We can all do our bit by spreading the word, increasing awareness about how to camp responsibly, and the potentially devastating effects of getting it wrong. We can act as guardians – the eyes and ears of wild places – raising the alarm if we see anything untoward going on. Leaving no trace is an essential part of wild camping philosophy.

In 1987, following a rapid increase in population and interest in being outdoors, the United States Department of Agriculture Forest Service, working with the National Park Service and the Bureau of Land Management, created a No Trace programme for wilderness and backcountry travel. Recognising the importance of good practice to protect the wild areas of the USA, they distributed a pamphlet of Leave No Trace ethics. In the early 1990s, the National Outdoor Leadership School developed a science-based minimal impact training course for non-motorised outdoor activity leaders. From this, the non-profit charity Leave No Trace was formed in 1994 with the aim of providing well-researched information, principles and training for outdoor people and organisations to follow. Today, Leave No Trace provides information, research, education and consultation to individuals, companies, landowners and governments to help preserve outdoor space and access to the outdoors.

Leave No Trace has seven guiding principles for responsible outdoor camping and recreation, which are globally relevant for camping and all outdoor adventures:

1 Plan ahead and prepare.
2 Travel and camp on durable surfaces.
3 Dispose of waste properly.
4 Leave what you find.
5 Minimise campfire impacts.
6 Respect wildlife.
7 Be considerate of others.

We'd also add the following:

1 Take a bag to collect any litter you find dropped by others.
2 Quickly notify the relevant authorities should you see any high-risk activity, such as potential fire hazards, damage or nuisance to local land, wildlife or communities.

▼ Leaving no trace is an essential part of wild camping philosophy

A QUICK GUIDE TO CAMPING WITH KIDS

WAKING UP in a tent as the sun's rays warm the canvas; unzipping the entrance on to a spectacular view; breakfast outdoors and days spent adventuring and exploring... Family camping is an exciting and incredibly special shared experience. We've been taking our kids camping since they were just weeks old; in fact, regular camping trips have become an important part of our year. But it's been a steep learning curve, with many challenges that we've had to overcome along the way. Here are some top tips for happy family camping.

CHOOSE THE RIGHT TENT

The most important decision is – of course – which tent you're going to take camping. Your tent will be your home, shelter, bedroom, playroom and potentially your kitchen and dining room, too. It's worth having a really good look around and also speaking to any family and friends who already go camping –

▼ Fun family camping with Sierra Designs Twin Lakes Duo double sleeping bag and Fern Canyon tent

you could even borrow one for a week before you commit. Many shops have space to pitch tents or hold tent shows where you can walk around potential tents and try out what they're like inside. The main considerations are:

Size and layout

Depending on how many of you there are and your children's ages, your needs will vary, so think about the layout that will suit you best. Younger children may be happiest sleeping all in one space with you, whereas older ones might like their own bedrooms. Separate living and sleeping areas can be useful – keeping sticky fingers and muddy boots well away from bedding is always good! A porch or awning is a great way of adding a bit of extra space for cooking and keeping outdoor footwear, especially if it rains. When our children were younger, a bell tent worked perfectly as we had one big space for living, playing and sleeping. Now our children are older, we have a tent with a large central living space and separate sleeping pods so everyone can escape for a bit of privacy when required.

Fabrics

The tent's fabric will affect how weatherproof it is, how long it lasts, its weight and pack size, and what it will be like to live in. Family tents are made of either nylon or a cotton-based canvas: nylon is cheaper, lighter and packs smaller but a canvas tent will last longer, suffer less from UV damage and is more breathable – great for warm-weather camping.

Your tent will be your home, shelter, bedroom, playroom and potentially your kitchen and dining room, too.

Price

In general, the more you pay for a tent, the better it will stand up to use and the longer it will last. Family tents are often fairly large structures that catch the wind, so you may pay for a cheap tent but end up with broken poles and/or torn fabric. It's worth looking around at the end of the season for great bargains to take camping the following summer.

PITCHING IT RIGHT

- The first time you pitch the tent, you may find it takes longer than subsequent pitches. Try out a test pitch in the garden or the park and it will all feel much easier when you pitch it for real.
- Find as flat a spot as possible. Sleeping on a slope is uncomfortable and small children seem to manage to roll down even the gentlest of inclines.
- Use all of the guy lines and pegging points to ensure a good, strong pitch.
- Think about where the prevailing wind is coming from and how this will affect the tent. If you have a longer tunnel-type tent, pitch it pointing away from the direction

◀ A small helper handing out the pegs

but they're available for single-space tents (such as bell tents), too.

Sleeping bags

Sleeping bags vary mainly in their filling and shape. A down-filled bag will give you the best warmth for its weight and pack size, but they tend to be more expensive and are harder to clean. A bag filled with synthetic insulation will be bulkier and heavier but also cheaper and easier to look after. Some bags taper towards the feet, adding warmth and reducing weight and pack size, whereas others are a roomier cut for comfort. Make your choice depending on what's most important for your trip. Kids love having their own sleeping bags – with smaller children, it will be warmer for them to have a shorter, child-specific bag. If space isn't an issue, a normal duvet works perfectly well.

of the wind so that your entrance and porch are as sheltered as possible.
● Get the kids involved! They'll love to help build their new holiday home – from handing you pegs to putting the poles together, it's a great way to introduce them to the world of camping.

SLEEPING

An inner tent creates a warmer space for sleeping, particularly in a large tent. Most family tents come with these as standard

Sleeping mats

Airbeds are a popular choice for family camping and are comfortable, but can be cold if the ground is cold, and they take up a lot of room. Foam roll mats are small and lightweight but don't give you much in terms of comfort. Self-inflating mats combine the two and are well worth the investment.

Camp cots, which feature a lightweight metal frame and mesh sleeping platform, keep you off the ground. Because of their design, they're also great for keeping younger children in one place when they're prone to sliding off their sleeping mats. A sleeping mat laid on top of the cot adds extra warmth and comfort.

Camp cookery

Cooking while camping is often a fun and sociable affair. With small children around, it's important to choose a stove that's stable and can be positioned well out of the reach of little hands – a low, stable double-burner is a great choice. Get the kids involved with washing and chopping up veg and even doing some foraging. As long as you're confident in your ability to currently identify it, wild food is abundant in many parts of the world and makes a fantastic, healthy and free addition to many dishes.

EXPLORING AND ADVENTURING

Camping is a great way to introduce children to the joys of the natural environment. Many campsites have on-site playgrounds, which allow the kids plenty of outdoor play, freedom and socialising, often within sight of the tent.

Choose a campsite that's in an area you'd like to explore: the beach, woodland, mountains or rivers all make perfect natural playgrounds for children of any age. Get older children involved in planning your adventures, but make sure you limit their choices to two or three options or it can feel a bit overwhelming. Pack a picnic and show them on a map where you'll be stopping for lunch or find a cafe to walk to; kids don't really understand the concept of just walking for fun, so it's good to give them a goal that doubles as a reward for their efforts. Once you're out, it's also important not to rush them too much if possible, allowing them to learn through playing, from skimming stones and climbing trees to simply watching a bee buzzing between flowers.

It's a good idea to have a means of carrying younger children comfortably and safely on rougher terrain. There are many different child carriers on the market that are designed exactly for this job. Soft carriers such as those made by Ergobaby are small and lightweight and can be carried in a rucksack when not in use. They keep your child's weight as near as possible to your centre of mass, which feels stable and comfortable. Most also have a range of positions, including front-facing inwards and outwards, back and hip carriers.

Finally, take plenty of snacks and spare clothing with you so you're prepared for hungry children, muddy socks, wet trousers or a change in the weather.

TOP TIP

SAFETY

It's extremely important to always cook in a well-ventilated area, well clear of the tent fabric.

What if it rains?

A rainy week camping might not sound like the most fun way to spend a holiday, but there's still plenty you can do that's enjoyable and family-friendly. Younger kids will happily spend hours splashing in puddles, so pack wellies for everyone. Wrap up warm, add a waterproof layer and head out to the woods if it's not too wet. Electric hook-up is available at many campsites, allowing you to plug in and power everything from mobile phone chargers and lanterns to camping kettles and small heaters. Having a readily available heat source is fantastic for camping in cold and/or wet weather, enabling you to dry out your family and your kit quickly and easily.

For many children, going on a camping trip can feel like a real adventure. It's not just going somewhere different; it's a whole way of living that's completely different from their everyday lives. It's also a great opportunity to have an adventure together as a family, disconnecting from established social and behavioural patterns. Time outside, time together, the opportunity to meet and make new friends or to wander the fringes of the camping field spotting insects and wildflowers – it's a place where children can be happy in whatever way suits them. Spending many months living under canvas when our children were little taught us that many of the toys, screens and other forms of indoor entertainment are wonderfully irrelevant when you're camping.

A family camping trip can be a perfect way to spend time all together, away from the pressures and distractions of everyday life, in the great outdoors somewhere breathtakingly beautiful. And camping is good for us all: according to a recent study by Plymouth University, children who camp in the great outdoors at least once a year do better at school, and are happier and healthier, and that's

TOP TIP

FAMILY CAMPING

- Choose the right tent. Every family will have their own requirements – ask friends and camping shops, read reviews and, ideally, go along to a tent show to see the tents pitched before you decide.
- If it's the first time you've used your tent, have a practice run in the garden before you do it for real – it's nice to feel like you know what you're doing once you get to the campsite.
- Take some entertainment along with you – things like Frisbees, footballs, books and games are great for evenings at the campsite or rainy days.
- Get the kids involved with planning your trip – everything from which campsite and what activities to planning and helping to cook the meals.

definitely a recipe for happy parents, too!

Family camping's a sociable affair; we rarely see our kids when we're away camping on our favourite family-friendly campsite at the heart of Great Langdale in the Lake District. The family field is laid out so that the tents form a large circle around a wooded play area in the centre. Kids of all ages seem to get along well here, climbing trees and balancing on obstacles; or they can spend their days playing in the small stream that runs through the site. There are also lots of organised activities nearby that the whole family can get involved in, from ghyll scrambling and rock climbing to bushcraft and foraging.

▼ Mountain adventures during a camping trip in Eryri (Snowdonia)

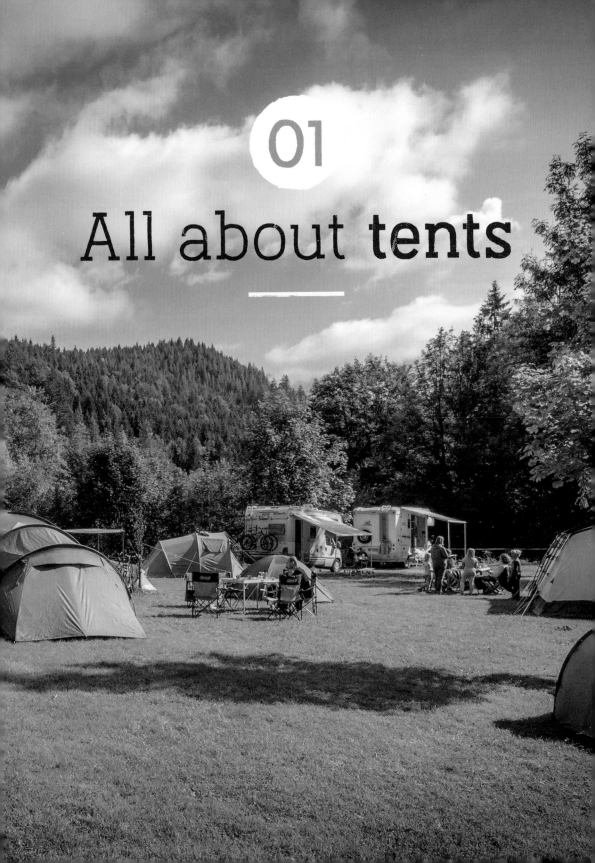

01
All about tents

Choosing the right tent

Tents come in many shapes and sizes; the 'right' one for you depends on a vast range of factors including budget, practicalities and preferences. If you're considering investing in a new tent, it's well worth visiting a tent show or a shop that has space to pitch them. That way, you can really get a 'feel' for each tent – what it's like inside and out, how the space and layout work, and what the experience of living in it for a week, a fortnight or longer will be like. If it's not possible to see your tent in real life before you buy it, many shops and brands produce short films enabling you to see in and around the tent and even watch it being pitched and packed away.

When choosing a tent, there are a few key considerations that will help to inform your final decision. Here are some of the most common.

Budget

Good tents don't come cheap but as long as they're well cared for, they should last for many years of adventures and can therefore be viewed as a long-term investment. A note of caution: while they might seem like a bargain, cheap, low-quality tents usually represent false economy. They may be treated with cheap but harmful chemicals, produced in factories with low wages and poor working conditions, and/or be made with low-quality materials and poor manufacturing techniques. The resulting tent, while costing less to buy, is likely to be less enjoyable to use, offer less weather protection and need replacing much sooner than a more carefully and responsibly made model.

Buying second-hand can be a brilliant way to pick up a tent or other outdoor kit for a bargain price. See the Resources section at the end of this book for some of the best places to look for second-hand kit.

If you're after a new tent, buying out of season or choosing an older version is another great way to save on cost. Brands often make minor updates to their tents, with new ranges being released at the start of the camping season each spring. Buying the previous year's model, and doing it at the end of the camping season or during the winter months, can save money. The same goes for outdoor clothing and footwear, which, as it is superseded by updated colours and designs at the start of each new season, can often be picked up for a fraction of its retail price.

Sharing expensive equipment with friends and family can also be a good way to afford better-quality equipment. Most of us only camp once or twice a year, so it makes sense to spread the use, and therefore the cost. It's also possible to rent tents and other equipment, especially the more specialist kind required for expedition and high-altitude use.

Do you really need a new tent?

Tents are designed to last and many people have an old one in the attic somewhere. Usually, it's the peripheral structures that break first – poles, pegs, zips and so on – and these are easily mended or replaced. Holes and tears in tent fabric can also be repaired relatively easily. Chapter 6 has a comprehensive guide to mending and maintaining your outdoor kit.

▼ Tents need to be large enough for you and your kit, but also portable – especially if you'll be carrying it

How many people?

▲ A lightweight cycle touring set up

Your tent needs to be large enough for everyone to live comfortably inside it during the day and night, for the duration of the trip, while still being pitchable, packable and portable. Wet-weather trips tend to require more indoor space, as it's likely you'll be spending more time under cover. Some tents have one large area for use as a combined living and sleeping quarters, while others have partitioned areas, or even separate pods, for sleeping.

It can be tempting to think more is better when it comes to living space but, especially if you'll be generally camping in good weather, you're likely to spend a lot of your time outdoors. Pitching an enormous tent can also be an adventure in its own right – especially if it's windy... If you're willing to sacrifice a bit of space, a smaller tent is likely to be simpler to pitch, easier and lighter to store and carry, and more weatherproof. A smaller main tent combined with a larger awning or standalone shelter can be a good way to add extra undercover outdoor space – that way, if the wind picks up you can simply pack the larger structure away. There's definitely a balance to be found between having plenty of indoor space in case of bad weather and having a tent that won't blow away.

If you're camping as a family, it's also worth taking a longer-term view and considering how your needs will evolve over the coming years. When our children were little, we all slept in one shared space on camping trips. Now they're bigger,

they enjoy sharing their own bedroom compartment, and it's nice for us to have our own, too. A couple more years down the line and they'll probably want their own rooms – and then their own tents! It's tricky to find just one tent that will accommodate many years of ever-evolving family requirements, but it's a great idea to consider how things might change a few years into the future if you can.

The durability of your tent is particularly important if you're planning to camp regularly or for longer stretches. Tents go through a lot each time they're put up and put down; even more so if the weather is bad.

While there are many variations, tents generally fall into the following three categories:

▼ The Nordisk Halland 2 LW offers plenty of space for a low weight and pack size, ideal for backpacking

▲ Cotton canvas bell tents are great for year-round family camping

Family tents

SPACIOUS AND DESIGNED for daily life for a larger number of people. Expect a roomy main compartment, separate sleeping quarters and a large porch for outdoor covered storage.

When you're choosing a family tent, think about how you'll use the space. If you're camping with younger children, a single large space often works well, so they can crawl or toddle about safely.

Bell tents work really well for this, and offer a cooler indoor space during hot weather due to their breathable cotton canvas fabric. Older children usually prefer their own space, so a tent with separate bedroom compartments is a good choice. Once they reach their teens they may even enjoy having a small tent of their own, pitched next to the main family tent.

▲ Lightweight three-person Vaude tent on a bikepacking adventure

Backpacking and lightweight tents

SMALL AND PORTABLE for ease of carrying and normally either solo, two or three-person. These tents usually feature one main living and sleeping area and a small porch to keep your boots and rucksack dry. In general, you'll need to sacrifice space if low weight and small pack size are your priorities, but otherwise, backpacking tents can be brilliantly versatile for everything from festivals, garden and car camping to multi-day adventures.

There are several different designs and materials available to suit specific needs and budgets, we'll discuss these further later in this chapter. The key points to think about when choosing a backpacking tent are weight, pack size, seasonality, durability, price, ease of set up and ventilation.

The best tent will suit your specific needs and the type of trips you plan to take.

Specialist tents

DESIGNED FOR SPECIFIC purposes, these tents tend to do one thing extremely well and will usually cost a premium as a result. Examples include highly wind-resistant tents for mountain use, super-lightweight tents for multi-day racing, tree tents and roof tents. Due to their specificity, these tents are usually lacking in versatility, so may not get a lot of use compared with a more general-purpose model. Consider carefully how often you'll use it, and if you could hire instead of buying.

▼ Sierra Designs Convert tent is designed for adventures in winter conditions

◄ Freestanding tents allow the inner to be pitched on its own. The flysheet can then be added or removed as required

The anatomy of a tent

All tents combine a weatherproof outer material with an inner structure, typically metal, fibreglass or air-filled beams. The specific materials depend on the type, use and cost of the tent.

Flysheet fabric

The flysheet is the outer layer of fabric, which provides the majority of a tent's protection from the elements. It can either be made from lightweight synthetic materials or heavier but more breathable cotton canvas.

Synthetic fabrics

Most modern tents use synthetic fabrics such as polyester and nylon. These materials are strong, light, have a small pack size and can be made to be very waterproof. Depending on their composition and quality, they can be used to make everything from budget tents for summer camping to high-performance, ultra-light or super-tough mountaineering tents.

The disadvantages of synthetic fabrics include being made from non-biodegradable plastics, and that unless specially treated, their performance will degrade over time due to exposure to UV light. Synthetic fabrics are also far less breathable than natural canvas, so the tents need to be well designed and ventilated to prevent condensation build-up inside – they can also become unbearably hot in warm weather. The seams need to be carefully constructed and usually taped to prevent them leaking. Many synthetic tents are treated with fire-retardant chemicals but they will still melt or burn if exposed to a flame so care should be taken when having a fire or cooking near the tent.

Some high-end lightweight and mountaineering tents use a silicone-coated nylon fabric such as silnylon. This is a strong nylon that has been treated on both sides with one or more coats of silicone to increase its tear strength. The result is a strong, light and highly waterproof fabric that feels smooth and slippery. While very effective, it's also expensive, so is only used on top-end tents where a high strength to low weight ratio is important.

Cotton

Traditional canvas tents, like bell tents, tipis and ridge tents, are made from heavy-duty cotton or polycotton. Though heavier and bulkier than synthetic fabrics, they offer better long-term durability – a result of being more resistant to UV damage and wear and tear. The fabric is more breathable, so natural fabric tents often feel far nicer to live in, especially in hot weather, and condensation is much less of a problem. They are also more naturally fire-resistant, meaning sparks from nearby fires are less worrisome. Larger canvas tents can even accommodate a wood burning stove with a flue – a hole is cut in the roof of the tent and fitted with a silicone-sealed metal flashing to allow smoke to escape well away from the living area without letting the rain in.

As well as the traditional tent designs, cotton or polycotton canvas is used for

▼ Cotton canvas tent set up

Waterproof ratings

WATERPROOF FABRICS are rated with a laboratory-based test to measure the Hydrostatic Head (HH) or waterproofness. This is a pressure test whereby a column of water stands on a tight piece of fabric, and the height of the water column that the fabric can withstand is the HH, measured in mm.

To be classed as waterproof, tent fabric must have a minimum HH rating of 1,500mm. Most tent fabrics have an HH of between 1,500mm and 6,000mm, with higher ratings meaning the fabric is more waterproof.

some modern family tents and, while they will be bulkier and heavier than synthetic versions, their natural longevity, fireproofing and breathability make them well worth considering for car camping. This kind of fabric is normally too heavy to be used for backpacking, although two-person tipi-style polycotton tents weighing in at around 3.5kg (7lb 12oz) are popular with

bushcraft enthusiasts who prefer to cook with an open fire.

Untreated cotton canvas is waterproof because when wet, the threads swell up, blocking any gaps in the fabric and preventing water from entering. When the fabric is touched – for example by the stray end of a sleeping bag resting upon it – the surface tension of the water is broken and the water is able to leak through. For this reason, it's a good idea to reiterate the importance of keeping everything away from the tent fabric during wet weather.

Canvas tents such as bell tents and tipis generally only have one main layer of fabric, rather than a flysheet and an inner. While this creates a wonderfully light, airy environment, the downside is a lack of insulation compared with a double-skin construction. Fantastic for both warmth and privacy, a bedroom tent, which hangs inside the main space of a bell tent or tipi, is a great way to divide up your space, keep living and sleeping areas separate, and add an extra layer of insultation. Which brings us nicely on to…

Inner tents

Most synthetic fabric tents feature a double-skin construction, combining a waterproof outer flysheet with a breathable inner made from a lightweight polyester or nylon with mesh panels. The inner is usually sewn into the groundsheet to create a sealed but breathable space. Some tents have a standalone inner tent that is pitched first and can be used on its own in warm, dry weather. Others have an inner tent that clips into the outer, allowing both to be pitched simultaneously. In small tents and some more specialist larger tents, the inner tent will take up almost the whole tent, but those designed for families or other groups have a range of different arrangements, sharing the available space between living and sleeping compartments.

An inner tent reduces the condensation that can form on the inside of the flysheet, keeps insects and other animals out, and traps warm air far more effectively than a single skin would – important for cold-weather camping. Bedroom tents can also be made from a blackout

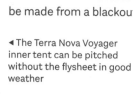

◄ The Terra Nova Voyager inner tent can be pitched without the flysheet in good weather

[34]

material, which may be a good idea if you, or anyone you're camping with, struggles with light mornings.

Some super-lightweight tents, such as those used for mountain marathons and fastpacking (trail running combined with backpacking), are a single-skin design in order to make them as light as possible. They inevitably sacrifice some comfort as a result and are best suited to a couple of nights at a time.

Groundsheets

The groundsheet protects campers and kit from wet ground, so it will be made from a durable, waterproof fabric. Most groundsheets in lighter tents are nylon, while heavy-duty tarpaulin fabrics are common in some larger canvas tents. A bathtub-style groundsheet is best for most scenarios, meaning the groundsheet comes up around the edges of the tent (like a bathtub) for maximum protection against rain, puddles and cold air entering the tent at sleeping level.

Poles

A good set of tent poles is a clever thing: strong enough to cope with weather conditions and the weight of the fabric, bendy and springy enough to provide the structure of the tent, yet as light and packable as possible for ease of storing

> For maximum protection against rain, puddles and cold air entering the tent, a bathtub-style groundsheet is best...

and transporting the tent. Most tents use folding poles made from sections of fibreglass, aluminium or steel connected with an elasticated cord, which are then unfolded and connected to construct the tent. Fibreglass is cheap and works well for smaller tents but can struggle to be strong enough for family-sized tents – it is liable to snap and when it does, it tends to splinter. Aluminium poles are light and strong – they often bend slightly, which isn't normally a problem, but they can also snap. Steel poles are strong but also heavy, so they're generally only found in larger, traditional-style tents when weight and pack size aren't so important. Some specialist tents use carbon fibre poles, which are both lighter and stronger than aluminium, but also more expensive.

Air beams

Family tents of all styles are increasingly using air beams instead of poles. These make pitching the tent easier, particularly if you're pitching on your own, as it simply

TOP TIP

AIR BEAM TENTS IN HOT WEATHER

When using air beam tents in hot weather, reduce the air pressure in the beams during the day to allow for expansion. Fully inflating the tent when you arrive late at night and then failing to let some air out as the temperature rises the following day can result in damage to the air tubes – they can even burst. You might need to pump them up a bit as the temperature reduces again in the evening.

needs laying out and then inflating. As long as it's well pitched, a good air beam tent can be very weather-resistant. In high winds, the beams can bend without damage when a metal pole would be more likely to break. Downsides include the risk of punctures, a single large and heavy package that can't be separated out into poles and main tent as a traditional tent can be, and the need for a means of inflating. A few smaller tents use air beams: they tend to be slightly heavier than an equivalent tent with aluminium poles but can pack smaller, so they're a good choice for bikepacking and kayak camping when poles may be awkward, but weight isn't as much of an issue.

contact. These are often included in 4-season tents when the force of strong winds pulling on the pegs can be considerable. Soft-ground pegs are also available, which are much wider and longer to give purchase in soft earth, sand or snow. Finally, steel rock pegs are used for pitching on hard, rocky ground, although not actually into rock.

It's easy to default to using the pegs that originally came with the tent, but if you know that the ground conditions you'll be camping on might be tricky, it's well worth investing in some more specific pegs. They'll be far more effective and much easier to use.

In all cases, pegs should be pushed in so they lean at an angle slightly away from the tent to give them the maximum hold in the ground. Pegs placed vertically or angled towards the tent can be more easily pulled out by a strong gust of wind.

Pegs

Tent pegs, which are usually made from metal, are driven into the ground to anchor the tent. Basic pegs are made from chunky steel wire with a hook shape at one end, to make it easier to pull them out and keep the guy lines in place, and they're standard in many smaller and cheaper tents. Lightweight aluminium wire pegs are sometimes used in 2- or 3-season backpacking tents where low weight is important. V- or U-shaped steel or aluminium pegs increase the surface area of the peg so they hold better in the ground and are often included with larger tents. Triangular Y- or X-shaped pegs are strongest and allow for maximum ground

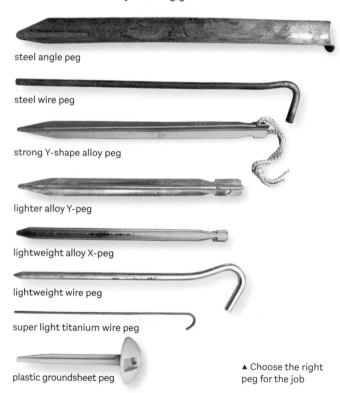

steel angle peg

steel wire peg

strong Y-shape alloy peg

lighter alloy Y-peg

lightweight alloy X-peg

lightweight wire peg

super light titanium wire peg

plastic groundsheet peg

▲ Choose the right peg for the job

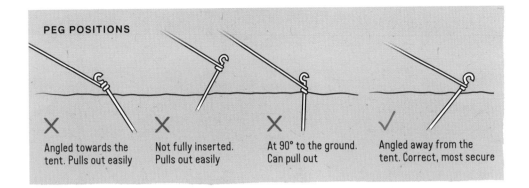

PEG POSITIONS

X Angled towards the tent. Pulls out easily

X Not fully inserted. Pulls out easily

X At 90° to the ground. Can pull out

✓ Angled away from the tent. Correct, most secure

Mallets

A mallet can be a handy item, especially if you're pitching on compacted ground, and even more so if you're likely to be wearing flip-flops. Most of the time, pegs can be pushed into the ground quite easily, sometimes with a bit of encouragement from the bottom of a walking boot. The pegs don't need to be completely buried so don't worry if they get most of the way in and then stick. On those occasions when no amount of pushing or other persuasion will sink a peg, a mallet can be highly effective, and save your hands and feet from injury. If you're using thinner wire-type pegs you may find they bend if you use a mallet, but they are great with the tougher styles of peg.

Guy lines

Guy lines are strong nylon cords that add pegging points from higher up on the tent and make it more secure in high winds. Some tents are free-standing and don't require guy lines for their structure, while others require the guy lines

to be pegged out in order to stand. Cord locks are normally added so that you can adjust the length of the guy line to suit the situation. Using all your guy lines and adjusting them correctly results in a tent that looks good, won't flap about (or worse) in windy weather, and is more pleasant to live in. It might feel like a faff to do, but it's well worth the effort.

Guy lines are a trip hazard. Some family tents use highly visible reflective guy lines but, as suggested previously, adding extra visibility, such as in the form of lights, to prevent trips is always a good idea.

Tent footprint

A footprint is an additional groundsheet made from a tough waterproof material designed to be placed under the tent, protecting it from wear and tear. It also adds extra waterproofing and insulation from the ground. Most tents have a specific footprint designed for their shape, which is easiest to use, but any tough, waterproof fabric could be used.

TOP TIP

USING A FOOTPRINT

If you're using a footprint, make sure it doesn't protrude around the sides of your tent as this can channel water underneath – you don't want to wake up in a puddle.

Which type of tent?

There are many different shapes, sizes and styles of tent, each one designed for a specific purpose. Your choice will be guided by:

- The number of people and how much kit you'll be camping with
- How, when and where you'll be using the tent
- Your budget
- Personal preferences around style, colour and layout

While each tent has its own set of specific features, tent designs generally fall into one of the following categories:

Tunnel tents

Pros

+ Steep walls create lots of internal space
+ Easy to pitch
+ Lightweight

Cons

– Not freestanding. Rely on pegs

TUNNEL TENTS are constructed from a series of parallel hoops. They are simple to pitch, lightweight for their size, and offer a good amount of inside space due to their vertical rather than sloping walls. They're not free-standing and require pegs to hold them up as well as to stop them blowing away, which can be challenging if you're pitching in windy weather or on very hard or soft ground. Tunnel tents are available in a range of sizes, from single-person through to large family tents that you can stand up in.

▲ Hilleberg Keron 4GT

Dome tents

Pros	
	+ Easy to pitch
	+ Budget friendly
	+ Freestanding

Cons	
	− Normally one door and one porch only
	− Will flex a lot in higher wind

THESE ARE SIMPLE two-pole tents for which the poles go from one corner to the opposite corner, crossing in the middle. They are free-standing and small models are easy to pitch, while larger dome tents can be more awkward due to their size. Dome tents are reasonably weatherproof, offer good internal space and are usually relatively light in weight. Some models come with an extra porch pole to extend the front and add some covered storage/sitting space. They can have one entrance, or an entrance at each end.

Smaller dome tents – those designed for two or three people – are a good, and often relatively low-budget option for those mainly camping in good weather. With their two-pole design, however, larger dome tents may lack the strength needed to cope with bad weather.

▼ MSR Elixir 2

Geodesic tents

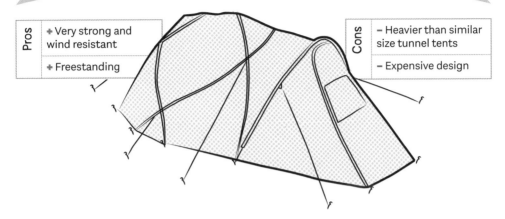

Pros	
+ Very strong and wind resistant	
+ Freestanding	

Cons	
– Heavier than similar size tunnel tents	
– Expensive design	

GEODESIC TENTS look similar to dome tents, but they have at least four poles, which cross each other in five or more places, creating a stronger and more stable structure. As a result, they're heavier, but excellent at coping with high winds and snow load, making them ideal for expeditions and winter adventures. Because of their strong, aerodynamic shape, the walls of geodesic tents slope inwards at a steeper angle than those of tunnel or dome-style tents. This reduces the internal space of the tent, especially standing height.

Geodesic tents are normally designed for two to four people, but larger expedition base-camp-style tents are available; these use a greater number of poles and pole crossing points to make very strong shelters for bigger groups, kit and equipment.

▲ Terra Nova Quasar tents

[41]

Semi-geodesic tents

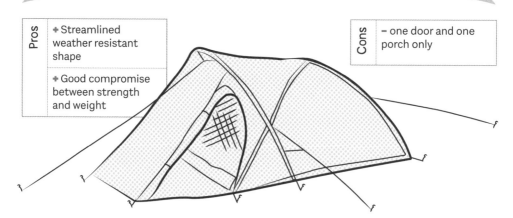

Pros

+ Streamlined weather resistant shape

+ Good compromise between strength and weight

Cons

− one door and one porch only

THREE-POLE TENTS combine the lighter weight of a dome tent with the added strength of an extra pole. Their streamlined design features a lower foot end rising to a higher front where the entrance and porch is, allowing you to sit up. Semi-geodesic tents are a good choice for year-round backpacking or lightweight winter camping, offering a good compromise between strength and low weight. They're available as two-, three- or four-person lightweight tents or as larger lightweight family-sized tents where the additional strength of the third pole makes them much more durable than similar-sized dome tents. Some semi-geodesic tents have a fourth pole to create a larger separate porch space.

▲ Vaude Hogan SUL

Single pole designs

Pros	
	+ Very light
	+ Easy to pitch
	+ Small pack size

Cons	
	− Low headroom
	− Single pole is not able to stand snow or high wind

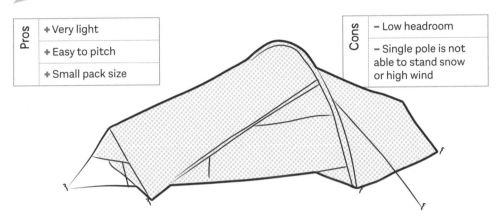

WHEN THE LIGHTEST possible weight and a tiny pack size are crucial – for example during racing, fastpacking, bikepacking or solo backpacking adventures – you might want to consider a tent with just one pole. The pole can either run across the length of the tent for a stronger and lighter design at the cost of some internal space, or along the length of the tent for maximum internal space to low weight. Single pole tents are usually designed for one or two people, as bigger tents need more structure. They have one entrance, either at the side or front, and a small porch space.

▲ Wild Country Zephyros 2

Ridge tents

Pros

+ Strong and durable
+ Lightweight versions can use trekking poles
+ Simple design

Cons

− No porch
− Steeply sloping walls reduce internal space

THIS IS THE CLASSIC vintage tent design with an upright pole at each end and a ridge pole between them. They're perhaps not as practical as some other tent designs, but they do look very cool with their old-school vibe and clean, simple lines.

Ridge tents are both breathable and highly weatherproof, but their sloping sides reduce the amount of usable internal space compared with some other styles. Most ridge tents require strong but heavy steel poles to support the shape, but some modern ultra-light tents utilise the ridge tent design using trekking poles to pitch – an innovative weight-saving strategy if you'll be carrying trekking poles anyway. You can have an entrance at each end, but there's not typically much of a porch area.

▼ Vango Force 10

Pop-up tents

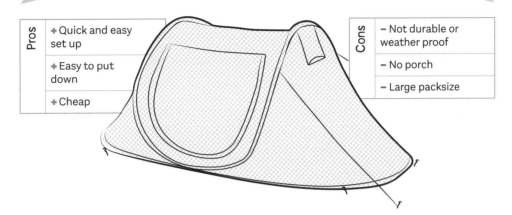

Pros
+ Quick and easy set up
+ Easy to put down
+ Cheap

Cons
− Not durable or weather proof
− No porch
− Large packsize

SPRINGING UP when you take them out of the bag, smaller pop-up tents assemble themselves in a matter of seconds but packing them away again can take a little longer. Pop-up tents stay fully assembled with the fabric and poles remaining connected when you put them away. This has its advantages in simple, rapid pitching but tends to create a larger pack size that means they're only suitable for car camping, garden and festival use. The design is also not as strong as most other styles, so they don't cope well with higher winds or bad weather. Most pop-up tents are designed for one to four people. Larger pop-up tents are available, but these tend to involve a bit more assembling as the poles fold and lock into place rather than just springing open.

▲ Quechua pop-up tents, by Decathlon

Frame tents

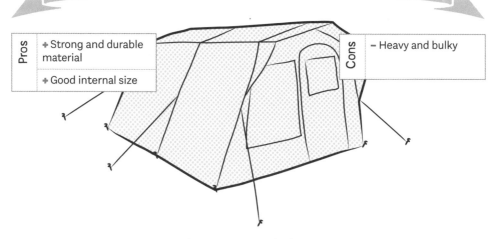

Pros
+ Strong and durable material
+ Good internal size

Cons
− Heavy and bulky

DESIGNED LIKE A MARQUEE, these traditional steel-frame tents have a large, open living space with near vertical walls to head height and a gently sloping roof. They are pitched by assembling the steel frame, pulling the fabric over the top of it and then securing it down, which can be hard work and takes longer than the more portable tent designs. These tents are also heavy and bulky and, although strong, the vertical walls will feel the brunt of any strong winds. Only available as large family campsite tents.

▲ Slapton Sands Camping and Caravanning Club site

Bell tents

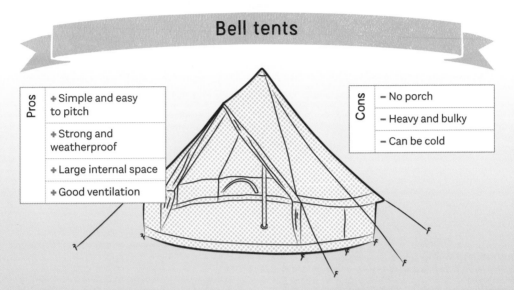

Pros

+ Simple and easy to pitch
+ Strong and weatherproof
+ Large internal space
+ Good ventilation

Cons

– No porch
– Heavy and bulky
– Can be cold

IF YOU'RE LOOKING for a family-sized tent, traditional bell tents offer a good compromise between living space and pack size, and they are easy to pitch and very weather resistant. The vertical wall around the base creates much more internal living space than a tipi of the same diameter. Single pole-design bell tents are available from 3–6m (9.8–19.6ft) diameter, sleeping up to eight people. Double pole 'emperor' bell tents are also available, sleeping around ten people, but these are less stable in windy conditions than the traditional round design – as we once discovered when ours blew down during windy weather on the south coast of England.

Bell tents are almost always made from cotton or polycotton canvas with heavy-duty groundsheets. This means they're a joy to live in, letting air and daylight in better than a synthetic tent, and they're more durable, too. As discussed above, an inner bedroom tent is a worthwhile addition to a bell tent, adding warmth, privacy and the ability to separate living and sleeping quarters.

The main downside of bell tents is that they're heavy and bulky, meaning they're best suited to those occasions when they don't need to be carried far, such as garden and car camping.

▼ Canvas bell tent at Bryher campsite, Isles of Scilly

Tipis

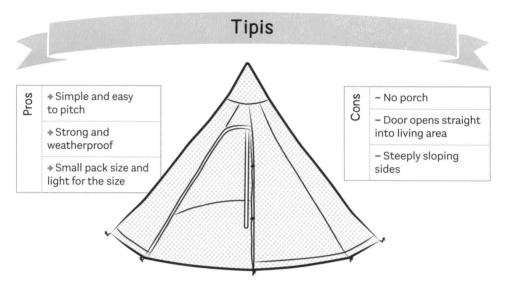

Pros	
	+ Simple and easy to pitch
	+ Strong and weatherproof
	+ Small pack size and light for the size

Cons	
	– No porch
	– Door opens straight into living area
	– Steeply sloping sides

THE TIPI is a traditional triangular tent with a single central pole or several poles running from the edge to the top. Tipis are easy to pitch, have a fairly small pack size and resist the weather well thanks to the sloping, rounded walls. Lightweight two-person tipis made from synthetic fabrics weigh less than 2kg (4lb 7oz), making them a viable backpacking option. Larger tipis are made from a cotton or polycotton canvas, with a single centre pole up to a 6m (19.6ft) diameter, and sleep up to 15 people. As with natural canvas bell tents, these are very durable and breathable, making them a good option for warmer weather or longer-term camping. The single centre pole design is the quickest to pitch and keeps the pack size manageable. Huge event-style tipi marquees are available that can seat more than 70 people.

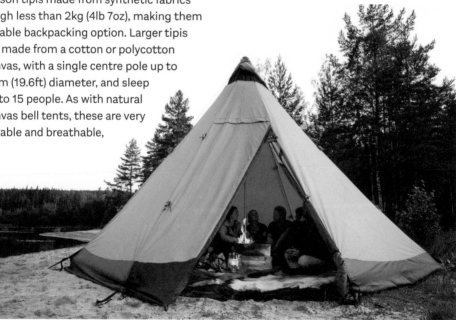

▲ Tentipi Safir 9 CP in Sunne, Sweden

Bivis, bedrolls, tarps and hammocks

Bivi bags

In its simplest form, a bivi bag is a waterproof cover for your sleeping bag. Bivvying offers the ability to really sleep out in the wild, unencumbered by even a tent, and can be done very subtly, simply bedding down behind a wall or hedge, invisible in the midst of the landscape. Bivi bags are very light, packable and portable, making them ideal for solo trips when you don't need the shelter or privacy of a tent.

▲ Bivi bags are a simple and lightweight option for solo camping

Basic bivi bags can be made from non-breathable plastic, but even the so-called breathable versions won't let in enough air for comfort, especially if it's raining. Most bivi bags have a zip, allowing you to close out the weather, and some have an insect-proof mesh that you can zip closed without having to fully seal the bag. Always leave the zip open a little to allow easy breathing and reduce the condensation build-up that can mean your sleeping bag is soaked through by morning. Some bivi bags have a short single pole to hold the material away from your face, which is more comfortable but bulkier and heavier. While placing your sleeping mat on the ground with your bivi bag on top probably works best when it's dry, some bivi bags have room to put your mat inside, giving you the option of keeping your mat dry on damp ground.

Bedrolls

Bedrolls are originated from horse-riding ranchers and shepherds who needed a durable and compact sleep system that was quick to deploy and repack. A bedroll consists of a waterproof outer, a bit like a bivi bag, with a sleeping bag and sleeping mat inside. When you get up, you simply roll the whole thing up together into a weatherproof roll and strap it on to your horse.

Like bivis, bedrolls give you an unadulterated wild sleeping experience. They're quick to deploy, comfortable, warm, and if the weather's good, you can doze off while watching the stars. Modern waterproof bedrolls will cope with any weather; some have a pole over the head end to keep the fabric off your face and reduce the sense of claustrophobia if you're out in bad weather.

Commercial bedrolls come either with an integrated sleeping bag, or just as a shell so you can use your own. Most bedrolls have a sleeve for a sleeping mat so it always stays

in place, but you can also use a bedroll on a camp cot if you prefer. Those made from natural fabrics, including a traditional cotton canvas outer, are highly durable, create a pleasant internal environment for sleeping in, and are far more fire-resistant than polymer-based fabrics such as nylon and polyester – an important consideration if you'll be sleeping around a campfire.

Bedrolls are still popular in bushcraft circles and when travelling by horse, motorbike, boat or vehicle but they're probably too heavy and bulky to be used backpacking or bikepacking.

You can even make your own bedroll, customising it to suit your specific requirements using a sleeping mat of any design, a large rectangle of weatherproof canvas and a blanket. If it's colder, use multiple blankets or a warmer sleeping bag.

◄ A tarp offers a simple, versatile and lightweight shelter. Hammocks (*pictured above*) allow you to sleep clear of the ground, well away from rocks, puddles and uninvited creatures

Tarps

Tarps are lightweight sheets of waterproof fabric that can be arranged in a number of different ways to create a simple, customisable shelter. A really handy, versatile addition to any camping set-up, tarps can be used in a variety of ways, adding extra protection to the porch of a tent, adding a porch to tents that don't have them, or creating a protected cooking or sitting area outside. We use ours all the time – whether we're camping or just need a portable shelter for the park or garden. A tarp can also work well pitched over a bivi bag, hammock or just a sleeping bag as a light and unobtrusive shelter.

Hammocks

Hanging out in the trees in a hammock feels like the ultimate way to end a day of adventures, and it's a wonderful feeling to rock gently to sleep suspended above the forest floor. Unlike a tent or bivi, though, achieving this does need a couple of strong points to secure your hammock between – relatively easy in woodland and forest but surprisingly tricky elsewhere.

Many good hammocks have an integrated insect net to keep insects and other animals out. Pitching a tarp above the hammock using a cord strung between the hammock's attachment points as a support creates a private, sheltered space.

To sleep well in a hammock, position yourself diagonally across the fabric, rather than lying end-to-end. This allows you to lie as flat as possible, which is far more comfortable than lying in the banana shape of the hammock. Maximising the flat area of the hammock for your head and body, you'll probably find your feet rest slightly higher than your head. To reduce any resulting knee discomfort, try bending one leg and putting your foot under the other knee, or pop a jacket under your knees to support the joints and stop them from hyperextending.

Tree tents

Tree tents look very cool but they're quite niche and don't come cheap. Essentially a tent suspended between three trees or other strong attachment points rather than being pitched on the ground, they have a waterproof flysheet included. Unlike a hammock, the strong floor material and triangular arrangement create a flat platform, which is very comfortable to sleep on. As with the hammock, however, finding three appropriately placed trees isn't always easy so, unless you have ready access to woodland where you're allowed to camp, they may not be a worthwhile investment.

▼▶ Tree tents use three attachment points, combining the space of a small tent with the convenience of a hammock, as long as there are plenty of trees about. Tentsile's tree tents are fun, functional and eye-catching

Pros	
+ Fun and exciting to pitch and sleep in	
+ Comfortable and always flat	
+ Bug and animal protection	

Cons	
– Expensive	
– You need three suitably placed trees	

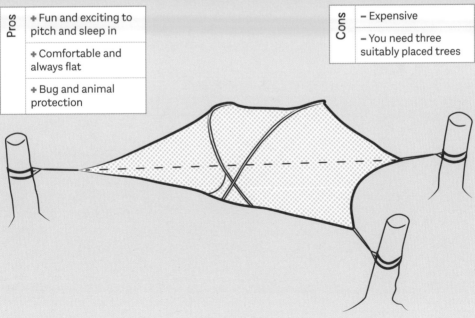

Roof tents

Designed to open out of a box attached to the roof bars of a vehicle or trailer, roof tents have a solid base with fold-out sections and additional support poles for extra space. Roof tents are expensive, but they're tough, convenient and quick to set up – the mattress and bedding can usually stay in the tent when you fold it away so it's ready to go for the next evening. They're a good choice for vehicle-based expeditions in areas where the ground is rough or rocky. Being off the ground on top of your vehicle, they also add protection against animals and insects, but this makes them far less suitable if you'll be camping with kids or dogs. Different models can sleep one to four people.

▼ Thule's Approach design takes rooftop tents to the next level, offering more space, more comfort and more adventures. Photo taken at 42,45010° N, 1,85699° E, Spain

▲ Terra Nova Quasar

The perfect pitch

Where and how you pitch your tent makes all the difference to both how your tent performs and the experience of living in and around it. Here's how to locate your perfect pitch and prepare the ground before you consider unpacking your tent.

1 Choose your spot

- The flatter the area on which you pitch your tent, the better. Everything from cooking and eating to sleeping is easier and more enjoyable on flat, level ground.
- Avoid water-logged ground or dips and hollows where puddles are likely to form in wet weather.
- Particularly if you're camping in exposed or weather-affected areas, choose a pitch that's as sheltered as possible from the prevailing wind.
- Campsites are usually very safe places, but be aware of hazards such as overhead powerlines, resident wildlife and other animals, and older trees that may be prone to dropping branches, particularly in windy weather.
- If you're wild camping, consider all the above plus any other potential hazards specific to the area. Camping close to a stream is handy for water but may flood in wet weather and attract animals and biting insects. Similarly, if you're camping on a beach, make sure you're well above the high tide line.

2 Prepare the ground

- Walk over the area, carefully checking for anything that might cause damage to your tent or discomfort to its inhabitants. Sticks, brambles, stones and old tent pegs are the usual suspects.
- Stamp down any molehills or other lumps and bumps as best you can.

3 Position and orientation

- When deciding on the orientation of your tent, the important things to consider are privacy, protection from the prevailing wind and, of course, the views you want to wake up to each morning.

▼ Consider the weather conditions and wind direction when pitching a tent, especially in exposed locations

- Ensure the main entrance to the tent is angled away from both the prevailing wind and anyone you don't want to have a view straight into your bedroom. On campsites where either of these is difficult, it's worth investing in a tarp or porch that can be angled to allow the greatest amount of wind protection and privacy.
- Great views straight from the tent are brilliant, and part of the appeal of camping, so should definitely be considered when choosing a pitch, but shouldn't take priority over any of the above points. Coastal campsites are a classic for this, when a sea view often means an accompanying brisk sea wind.
- Leaving a flat patch of ground in front of your tent gives you an area in which you can eat and enjoy the surroundings.

With the ground prepared and the positioning and orientation of the tent decided, it's time to get down to pitching. Every tent is slightly different to pitch, but the general approach is the same. Always follow the instructions for your specific model, but the following steps will help to make sure you're pitch perfect every time:

1. Take everything out of the main bag and check it's all there.
2. Spread out the main part of the tent – the part the poles insert into. Air beam tents will usually have the beams ready fitted.
3. Orientate the tent so that the main entrance is positioned away from the direction of the prevailing wind, as discussed above, and make sure all zips are done up.
4. Peg out the two points at the end of the tent that will be facing into the wind – this will prevent the tent blowing away as you continue to pitch it.
5. If your tent uses poles rather than air beams, assemble all the poles and then thread the main poles through the pole sleeves, loops or clips. If the poles are different lengths or shapes, they are usually colour coded for ease of use.
6. Starting at the pegged end, fit the ends of the poles into their corresponding anchor points on either side of the tent fabric, creating the main structure as you do so.
7. Peg out the corners, taking care to find the optimal direction and tension of each anchor point. Wrinkles, folds, asymmetry, straining and flapping of the tent fabric can all indicate a problem with the direction and/or tension of a peg placement.
8. Add any extra poles and, if part of the tent design, put the flysheet over the top.
9. Peg out the tent flaps (double-check the zips are done up before doing this).
10. Peg out guy lines and other peg points.
11. Many tents will have an integrated groundsheet, but those supplied separately should be clipped in at this point.
12. Hang any inner tents.
13. To take your tent down, reverse these instructions but ALWAYS PUSH TENT POLES, never pull them, as they'll come (frustratingly) apart.

Specialist pitching

On some adventures, you will want or need to pitch your tent on ground that's too soft or too hard for normal pegs. In this section, we'll discuss strategies for dealing with and pitching on solid rock or ice and soft sand or snow.

Sand and other soft ground

If you need to pitch on sand or other soft ground, standard tent pegs probably won't anchor your tent adequately. In this situation, self-supporting dome or geodesic-style tents will be easier to use than tunnel tents, as you just need to anchor them to stop them blowing away rather than to hold them up.

You can get much wider soft ground pegs, which will give more purchase and may allow you to pitch normally. There are a few other options that you can fashion from materials that are likely to be available: sticks or planks can be used as wider pegs, or you can tie the guy ropes to the midpoint of a stick or plank and bury it. You can

▲ Freestanding dome tent pitched on a rocky outcrop using rock anchors

create ground anchors by filling a bag with sand (stuff sacks and drybags work well), attaching it to a guy line and then burying it.

Rocks

Pitching a tent directly on rock can look spectacular but it's not great for the groundsheet. If you know you will be pitching on rock, a groundsheet protector, or a piece of tough tarpaulin, will help your tent last longer. We'd also recommend a full-length foam camping mat under your preferred self-inflating or blow-up air mat to add warmth and reduce the possibility of punctures.

Free-standing tents are much easier to pitch on rock than tunnel tents. You can't use pegs so you will need to anchor the tent by tying it to rocks or other anchor points.

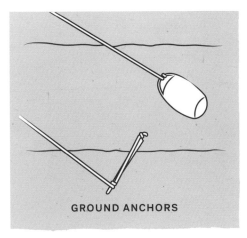

GROUND ANCHORS

SNOW

Top tips for pitching a tent in snow:

1 Be prepared for winter conditions, taking extra food and clothing with you. Pack a lightweight snow shovel and snow pegs as well as your usual camping kit and consider an extra layer of insulation either under or on top of your usual sleeping mat.

2 Avoid pitching below slopes prone to avalanching or where wind-blown snow will accumulate, for example too close to a boulder or a wall.

3 Keep your gloves on as much as possible and avoid touching metal objects such as pegs and shovels with bare skin.

4 Stamp down an area of snow a little larger than the footprint of your tent. You can also use a snow shovel at this point to level out your pitch – especially if it's on a slope. If you can, leave your flattened-out surface to harden up for a while before pitching your tent.

5 In shallower snow, you may be able to use your pegs as normal, pushing them through into the earth below. In deeper snow, you may need to bury your pegs horizontally with the guy lines tied on, stamping down the snow over the top to secure them.

6 Ice axes and trekking poles can double as additional pegs in deep snow, or you can use deadman anchors – tie guy lines around rocks or logs, dig a hole a short distance away from the tent where you want the anchor point to be and bury them, filling in the hole and stamping the snow down well.

7 In high winds, building up the snow around the edges of your tent helps to prevent the wind from getting in under the flysheet.

8 In heavy snowfall, be aware of snow accumulating on top of your tent or outside the entrance – get up and clear this away as regularly as required.

▲ Freestanding dome tent staked out in the snow

Ice

Pitching on ice is a bit like pitching on rock but you can use ice screws to anchor the tent as well as weighing it down with rocks. Here are the three commonly used methods:

1 If you have enough ice screws, simply use these instead of pegs and attach the tent to them.

2 If you don't have enough ice screws, you can drill holes in the ice at an angle away from the tent and then insert normal pegs into the holes, then tie the tent to them. This works best with longer and wider pegs – if they fit in the holes.

If you intend to leave the tent pitched during the day and use either of these methods, it's best to bury the pegs in snow or cover them in some way. This stops the anchors melting out when the sun warms the metal pegs or ice screws.

3 To avoid leaving any metal in the ice, you can cut Abalakov threads at each anchor point. These are V-shaped holes created by drilling two ice screws at oblique angles into the ice. Thread the loops created using cord and a hook made from some wire (specific Abalakov threading tools are available to buy) and tie the tent down using these loops.

Five weeks on ice

SIM: *'In 2004, I spent five weeks in Iceland with the British Exploring Society. We spent almost every night of the trip camping in tough Terra Nova Hyperspace tents, which stood up well to the gravelly terrain, high winds and lack of shelter. But I particularly remember the week a small group of us spent camped high up on the ice cap, where we taught the young explorers skills such as crevasse rescue and ice axe arrest in preparation for our ascent of the nearby mountain, Snæfell. Our tents were pitched directly on the ice, using a combination of rocks and ice screws to anchor them against the wind. I had a good sleeping bag and four of us slept in a three-person tent to help us stay warm, but it was the quality of our sleeping mats that made the most difference. Even so, lying directly on the ice with only a couple of layers of nylon and a three-quarter-length, 2.5cm (1in)-thick, self-inflating mat between me and the second largest ice cap in Europe was chilly! To add to the discomfort, our bodies melted the ice directly under us, so we created body-shaped depressions that quickly became shallow puddles. We had to move the tents frequently and cut drainage ditches around and under them to allow the meltwater to run off. It was an amazing experience, although we were all sleep deprived by the end. And it was the best lesson in how quickly we lose body heat through conduction – and the importance of a good-quality sleeping mat.'*

ABALAKOV THREAD

Additional shelter –
Tarps, porches, gazebos and windbreaks

Tarps, gazebos and windbreaks can be used to customise a camp set-up, adding weather protection, privacy and extra undercover space.

Tarps are brilliantly versatile, lightweight, waterproof square or rectangular sheets of tent fabric. Eyelets spaced along their edges and at the corners, enable a cord to be attached for pitching. Some come with their own pole(s), while others can be set up using existing tent poles, walking/running poles and even kayak paddles.

They also function as a standalone shelter, or a separate undercover area for

Five great tarp set-ups

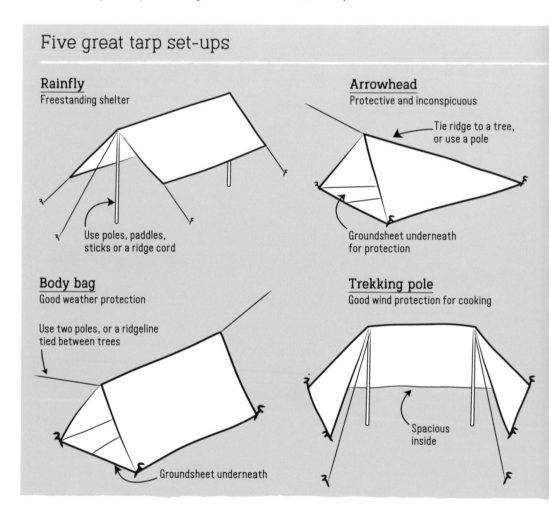

Rainfly
Freestanding shelter

Use poles, paddles, sticks or a ridge cord

Arrowhead
Protective and inconspicuous

Tie ridge to a tree, or use a pole

Groundsheet underneath for protection

Body bag
Good weather protection

Use two poles, or a ridgeline tied between trees

Groundsheet underneath

Trekking pole
Good wind protection for cooking

Spacious inside

cooking, eating or storage. Gazebos are free-standing shelters, which are more robust but heavier and less portable than tarps. Some have zipped sides so they can be fully enclosed if required. Event shelters tend to be larger, more weatherproof gazebos, often used for races and other events to offer privacy and weather protection.

Beach-style windbreaks can also be used to shelter the entrance to a tent from the wind, add privacy, or as a wall or divider.

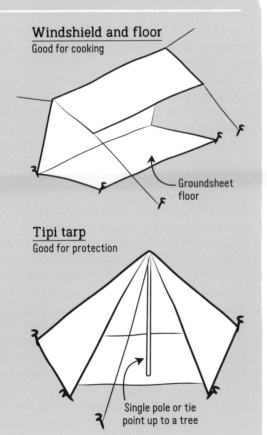

Windshield and floor
Good for cooking

Groundsheet floor

Tipi tarp
Good for protection

Single pole or tie point up to a tree

TOP TIP

CHOOSING A TENT AND PITCHING

1 The best tent for you is the one that suits the way you camp. Specialist tents might look cool, but they often lack versatility. If you start camping more often and need another tent for different conditions or circumstances, you can always add to your collection later.

2 Good tents don't come cheap, but they will last far longer and be far nicer to camp in than poorer-quality versions. If you're on a limited budget, buy out of season or look at ex-demo or second-hand options. A lightly used, high-quality tent is better than a new lower-quality one.

3 Practise pitching your tent and using any specialist pitching techniques somewhere safe and easy before your trip. You don't want to pitch a tent for the first time in howling wind and rain, or discover too late that the ground anchor technique you planned to use doesn't work with the kit you have.

4 Always take the time to think about the ground, nearby hazards and the weather, including the strength and direction of the wind. What happens if the weather changes markedly during your stay?

5 Tents work best and are the most fun to live in when they're pitched well, without bits that sag or flap about. Always use all the guy lines and pegging points.

02

Where to camp

Once you have your shelter sorted, whether that's one brilliantly versatile tent for all uses or a selection of more specialist models, it's time to decide where to go. Camping gives you the ability to experience places in an entirely different way to more self-contained campervans, caravans and holiday homes. You'll be right in the midst of the place, able to fully experience the sounds, sights and smells of your surroundings. You'll make connections, falling into conversation with those you meet, stumbling upon wildlife, synchronising with the natural rhythms of night and day. It's like having the best seats in the house.

Campsites

Established campsites are by far the most straightforward choice, all set up ready for you to arrive, pitch your tent and enjoy your holiday. Whether you love the buzz of a social campsite, you're keen to find a place where the kids can roam free or you prefer something a little more peaceful and out of the way, there are campsites to suit every taste.

Our checklist for the perfect campsite is lengthy: widely spaced, flat pitches; glorious views from the tent entrance; pristine facilities; space for the kids to run around; and somewhere nearby for fresh croissants each morning. It sounds like a lot to ask for, but it's surprising how often campsites manage to tick most of these boxes, and often add in a few extra ones, too.

Camping is hugely popular across much of Europe and, with over 28,000 campsites to choose from, it's a great way to explore and experience different countries and cultures. The most popular camping destinations are France, the UK, Germany, the Netherlands and Italy, but there are outstanding campsites to be found throughout the continent. In fact, some of the very best camping experiences can be found in the Nordic countries, where rich biodiversity (but few dangerous creatures), an abundance of beautiful wild places, and a well-established camping culture exist. Mainstream European campsites are generally well organised, with clean facilities, but size and standard vary widely so it's well worth doing some research before you travel or else be prepared to be flexible. Many sites accept a mixture of tents, campervans and caravans, but there are also plenty of smaller, tents-only sites for the purists.

Camping is also popular in the USA, where most campsites are federal- and state-managed, located in national forests, national parks and waterways, and have facilities such as showers, drinking water, electric hook-up and playgrounds. There are also many private campgrounds, ranging from back-to-basics wilderness camping to those equipped with swimming pools, Wi-Fi and shops.

◄ Windermere Camping and Caravanning Club site

▼ Pencelli Castle Caravan and Camping Park

Pop-up campsites

Pop-up campsites fill the gap between permanent campsites and legal wild camping. The definition varies worldwide with individual countries' or states' planning regulations, but essentially pop-up campsites are small and basic areas that are allowed to operate as a campsite for a limited amount of time each year. In the UK, landowners can use a field or other suitable area as a commercial tent-only campsite for up to 28 days per year, provided that they don't have to physically alter the site. There's no limit to the number of tents that can be accommodated and facilities may be available, but check before you go.

A pop-up campsite can help spread the load of a busy peak season in a popular location, allowing campers more choice and helping farmers and landowners gain a bit of extra income.

▼ Bell tents ready pitched and awaiting your stay

▶ The Lost Meadow Treepod at Wildish Cornwall

Glamping

If you like the idea of camping but perhaps want some extra luxury for a special occasion, or you don't want to carry a tent, or you're keen to try a specific tent or even the idea of sleeping in a tent without taking the plunge and buying one, glamping might be for you. It's also a great way for seasoned campers to get their less-keen friends and family to give it a go.

The wonderful – and sometimes slightly weird – world of glamping has allowed the imagination of those involved to run wild. Glamping is available in almost any structure you can think of: buses, helicopters, horseboxes, treehouses, planes and trains, as well as the more usual bell tents, yurts/gers, shepherds' huts and traditional caravans.

Bothies, huts and refuges

IN MORE REMOTE AREAS, such as the Scottish Highlands and mountainous regions of Europe, shelters have existed for a long time, offering those travelling through a refuge and a place to sleep. These may be free, particularly in the case of bothies and huts, or charge a small amount for board and often meals, such as is common in Alpine refuges. This kind of accommodation ranges from very basic to relatively luxurious. Even if you're travelling somewhere you intend to use this kind of shelter for your overnight stops, it's worth taking along a lightweight tent in case they're full. Many are happy for those unable to get a bed to camp nearby and still use the facilities.

Wild camping

With the right approach, wild camping can be the ultimate freedom. There's nothing quite like spending the day wandering through a beautiful landscape and then, as the sun begins to drop in the sky, simply finding a good spot and pitching your tent for the night. It's an incredible way to see and really experience new places on a budget, particularly if you can head for countries – or areas within countries – where wild camping is permitted, or even actively encouraged.

Wild camping works best for solo campers, couples or very small groups, preserving the specialness of the experience and minimising disruption to places and their resident people and wildlife. Part of the magic of wild camping lies in its ability to be almost invisible, allowing humans to be an integral part of the landscape rather than visiting tourists. In keeping with this ethos, leaving as little evidence of your stay as possible and living lightly on the land is essential. Forage sparingly, arrive late and leave early, be part of the peace and tranquillity of a place. Avoid campfires unless they are expressly permitted and, if you do need to heat water or food, use a stove that's well off the ground, stable and windproof. Some areas specifically prohibit the use of any open flames, including camping stoves, if there is a high fire risk, so take note of any signs. As well as the potential for scarring the land, poorly managed small fires can easily be the cause of devastatingly large ones.

TOP TIP

WHERE TO CAMP

1 It's best to plan ahead if you are staying in campsites, especially in high season, when they're likely to be full. If you can, book in advance and check the facilities. Do they take cards or is it cash only? Do they have electric hook-up and if so, do you have the correct style of cable?

2 If you plan to wild camp, check the rules in the area in which you are camping. Have a look at maps and decide on some possible campsites but be ready to adapt your plan and be flexible if you turn up to find your preidentified spot is already occupied or unsuitable.

3 Take a tent that matches the specifics of the place you're going to camp in. Campsites often charge according to the size of tent – worth bearing in mind if you're taking a big family tent along and there are only two of you. If you're wild camping, tents must be small and discreet.

Where can I wild camp?

Europe

Wild camping is prohibited in many European countries, though there are plenty of exceptions. The Nordic countries – Sweden, Norway and Finland – see wild camping as a right, as long as it is done responsibly and respectfully and on public, rather than private, land. Sweden doesn't extend this freedom to those travelling by car and doesn't permit campfires or stays longer than two nights in any one place. Wild camping isn't legal in neighbouring Denmark, but there are many forests and other areas in the country where it is expressly permitted, so seek these out first if you're hoping for a free stay. While it is legal to camp on public land in Spain, most of the country is privately owned, and that which isn't is often inhospitable to campers, with rocky ground and thorny vegetation.

Wild camping laws vary across the UK. Scotland permits wild camping on most land that is not privately owned, in accordance with the Scottish Outdoor Access Code. Wales does not permit wild camping without prior permission from the landowner. In England, following a high-profile lawsuit in 2022 and subsequent successful appeal in 2023, wild camping is

If you're subtle in your approach you can in theory wild camp almost anywhere, but for the most immersive and enjoyable experience it's usually best to stick to where it's allowed, or to seek permission from the landowner to camp on their land. Illegal wild campers can be moved on or even fined – in Switzerland, for example, you can expect a 10,000 euro fine if you're caught.

▲ ▶ Wild camping laws and enforcement vary widely between countries and regions. Check the local rules before pitching your tent

expressly permitted on parts of Dartmoor, and it's possible that other national parks may follow suit.

Many people do wild camp in the UK, staying from dusk till dawn and leaving no trace, and no one is any the wiser. However, in recent years, instances of fly camping – large groups leaving equipment behind and causing damage to the land and wildlife as well as a nuisance to local people – have been on the rise, making it more difficult for everyone. Some enterprising organisations now offer 'nearly' wild camping, with a back-to basics feel and generally lower cost than traditional campsites.

Much of France, Germany and Italy have a similar approach, where wild camping is not legally permitted but is tolerated when done responsibly – and ideally invisibly. It's worth bearing in mind, though, that wild campers in these areas may be asked to move on.

Along with Switzerland, whose law enforcement officers have something of a reputation among climbers wild camping in order to get an early start on the mountains, strict laws prohibiting wild camping exist in the Netherlands, Hungary, Portugal, Russia, Croatia, Serbia, Greece, Bulgaria, the Czech Republic and Slovakia. Wild campers in these countries can expect to be moved on and/or heavily fined if caught.

USA and Canada

Unless otherwise marked, wild camping in the USA is usually permitted on public lands, which cover about 27 per cent of the country. They include national forests and grasslands, Bureau of Land Management lands and, in Canada, Canadian Crown land.

03
Tent life

Once you've made all the big decisions such as where to go, what to take, who to go with, and which tent suits you and your adventure best, it's on to the really fun bit. This is the everyday of camping, a simpler, outdoorsy way of life. Particularly if you're car camping – or even garden camping – tent life doesn't have to be uncomfortable or austere.

It's easy to make a tent feel homely without needing to fill it with 'stuff'. A few cushions add colour and comfort to your living space, while some fun bunting or twinkly lights brighten up the inside or outside of your tent. We take a couple of

small beanbags with us on longer trips as they're great for relaxing, reading or simply watching the world go by, offering a greater variety of sitting positions than a camping chair and being far nicer to sit on than the ground. A portable, rechargeable speaker is perfect for in-tent entertainment, useful for everything from chilled-out campfire tunes to audiobooks to keep the kids happy.

Whether or not to leave the screens at home is one for personal consideration. As freelance, remote workers, our laptops and phones complete with an unlimited data contract come with us on all our trips. While this might seem like a bind to the real world you're busy trying to escape, for us being able to take work with us brings a freedom of its own. A tablet can be invaluable for those rainy evenings in the tent when a film, watched from the cosiness of sleeping bags, can be just the thing.

Even if you're going super-light, there are plenty of things you can do to make your days and nights more comfortable and enjoyable, from packing a cheap foam roll mat to place between your bed and the ground to improbably light and packable but certainly not cheap chairs.

The rest of this chapter is all about the practicalities of camping. From sleeping bags to stoves, power packs to wash kits, there are a whole host of options to make camp life better.

GETTING A GOOD NIGHT'S SLEEP

TOP
TIP

● Make sure your tent is right for the conditions and well pitched. Poorly pitched tents are a source of worry – will they stay upright or collapse on top of you? They also tend to flap loudly as soon as the wind picks up – not ideal for a restful night's sleep.

● Choose a sleeping bag that's rated to the temperature you're likely to be sleeping in. Take extra blankets to add warmth and unzip your sleeping bag if you're too hot.

● Take the most comfortable sleeping mat you're willing to carry. Offering both cushioning and insulation, the right mat makes a big difference to comfort and sleep quality.

● Take time over choosing a flat pitch and preparing it before setting up your tent. That way, you're less likely to spend the night sliding downhill or lying on a molehill.

● If you're keen to get a good night's sleep, camp well away from noisy groups, loud machinery, bright lights, roads and the thoroughfare to the toilet block.

● Earplugs are very helpful if you are a light sleeper, especially in summer when the dawn chorus is likely to wake you earlier than you may like.

▲ A cosy bell tent, set up for a relaxed evening and a good night's sleep

▲ Foam roll mats are cheap, lightweight and versatile

A good night's sleep

If you're comfortable in bed, you're much more likely to get a good night's sleep than if you're cold, lying at an unnatural angle or restlessly trying to find a less bumpy bit of ground. There's little doubt that well-slept campers have the most fun, so it's worth doing everything you can to ensure a restful and reviving night.

When you're camping there are lots of factors with the potential to affect how you sleep. Some of them are easy to modify, others less so.

TOP TIP

FOAM ROLL MATS

If space allows, adding a cheap, lightweight foam roll mat under your normal sleeping mat adds protection from the ground for you and your mat and a surprising amount of extra warmth.

Sleeping systems

A sleeping system for camping includes your mat and sleeping bag, along with sleeping bag liners, pillows and even the clothing you're planning to wear overnight. If you're not using a tent, a waterproof bivi bag would also be considered a part of your sleeping system. Considering each component in light of your individual preferences, the limitations of weight and pack size, and the conditions you'll be sleeping in is essential when it comes to creating an overall sleeping environment that's as comfortable and conducive to a good night's sleep as possible.

What to sleep on – camping mats, beds and cots

Sleeping directly on the ground or on the groundsheet of your tent is often cold and always uncomfortable. Cold ground is an excellent conductor of body heat – far better than the air above – so sleeping mat choice is important, especially when camping in colder weather. A well-insulated mat with a lighter sleeping bag will feel warmer than a warm sleeping bag on a poorly insulated mat. Fortunately, there's a great range of camping mats available to suit every need and budget.

Sleeping mats vary in their construction and materials, and this combination will determine the mat's warmth, weight and packability. A thicker mat offers better protection from any lumps and bumps in the ground, but it isn't necessarily warmer. Even the thickest airbeds, filled with air alone, can become horribly cold as the air inside them drops in temperature. Self-inflating mats such as those made by Thermarest have an integrated layer of foam insulation, which makes all the difference, and this type of mat offers excellent warmth and comfort for a relatively small weight and pack size. However, if you do need to use a standard, non-insulated airbed in colder weather, adding a simple and inexpensive foam roll mat underneath will insulate it, and therefore you, from the ground.

For car camping or when space and weight aren't a problem, adding mattress toppers and sheets makes any style of mat more comfortable to sleep on. The toppers add extra insulation and comfort, while cotton sheets are far nicer to lie on than plastic camping mats – and they're much easier to wash, too.

During very warm weather, it's worth letting a little air out of air mats during the day. This will prevent damage caused by overinflation when the air inside expands due to the heat.

Which camping mat?

Type	Overview	Pros	Cons
Foam roll mats	A good budget option and great to use under an air-filled sleep pad. Best used to add warmth to airbeds or mats.	Cheap, durable, lightweight	Bulky, not very warm or comfortable
Self-inflating mats	A good compromise between comfort, pack size, warmth and weight. Can be inflated by mouth but it's best to use a mini pump or pump sack (basically a drybag with a pump attachment) to avoid moisture building up inside, which can cause mould. Best used for general camping and backpacking. Thicker models, such as Alpkit's 7.5cm (3in)-thick Dozer, feel luxurious to sleep on and are invaluable in cold conditions.	Comfortable, warm, durable and can be repaired	Heavier and bulkier than air mats.
Air mats	These specialist mats are very lightweight with a small pack size but they're often more expensive, less durable and can be crackly to sleep on due to the materials used. They can be inflated by mouth but, as above, it's best to use a mini pump or pump sack. Some air mats contain down or synthetic insulation to increase the warmth. Designed for when low weight and pack size are paramount.	Super-light, small pack size, warm and comfortable	Expensive, not as durable as other types and the material can be noisy
Airbeds	Classic-style camping airbeds are fairly comfortable and low-cost but are bulky, heavy and can be cold. Use foam mats underneath and a mattress topper on top, especially in cold weather, to get a warmer night's sleep. They require a foot, hand or electric pump to inflate. Best suited to car camping in warm weather.	Cheap, comfortable, most like your bed at home, can be repaired	Can be cold, especially if the ground is cold; bulky and heavy
Camp cots	Combining a lightweight metal frame with a fabric base, these beds allow you to sleep off the ground, which is great for camping on rocky terrain. The frame also stops you rolling off the sleeping mat in the night – perfect for fidgety kids! For optimal comfort, add a camping mat on top, otherwise they can be a little cold and hard.	Dependable flat and comfortable bed that keeps you off the ground. Durable (ultra-light versions less so), smaller pack size than airbeds	Relatively heavy, requires flat ground or the use of chocks, cold if used without a sleep pad/mat

What to sleep in – sleeping bags and quilts

For most people, sleeping bags go hand-in-hand with camping. But, as long as space isn't an issue, it's perfectly acceptable to bring your usual duvet, sheets and pillow. While it may lack some of the adventurous feel of snuggling into a sleeping bag, the pay-off is comfort, breathability, a greater ability to vary warmth, easy washing/drying and plenty of room to move your feet around. If you're camping with younger children, it's also much easier for them to snuggle in with you if they want to.

If you only ever car camp, using your existing bedding saves buying a sleeping bag that you may not use very often, or sleeping bags for children who may well have grown out of them within a year or two. Even if you do use a sleeping bag, it's a good idea to have a quilt or a couple of blankets on hand in case the temperature drops overnight.

Sleeping bags come in a wide range of styles to suit every occasion. At one end of the spectrum are the wide, rectangular-shaped cotton/polycotton bags with plenty of foot room, perfect for garden and car camping when the weight and space they take up doesn't matter. At the other end are slim-fit, mummy-shaped bags made

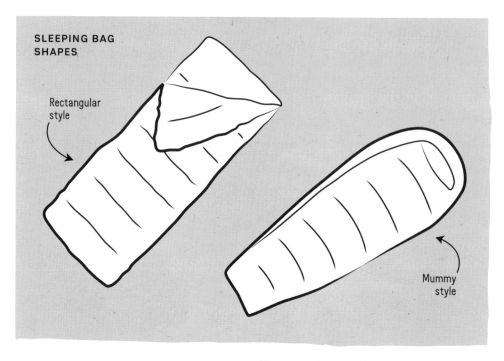

SLEEPING BAG SHAPES

Rectangular style

Mummy style

from technical fabrics that maximise the amount of warmth you get for a tiny weight and pack size. From breathable, lightweight, synthetic summer-weight bags to those stuffed with enough down to keep you alive in the arctic winter, there really are sleeping bags designed for every situation and environment. In the section that follows, we'll unzip the world of sleeping bags so you can choose the one that's right for you.

How to choose the perfect sleeping bag

Sleeping bags provide packable, portable warmth and comfort. The right bag for the conditions you'll be camping in can make the difference between a warm and comfortable night's sleep and a cold and sleepless one. In some environments, they can even save your life.

Temperature ratings

Sleeping bags are usually given a season rating, depending on how warm they are. While this isn't as specific as a temperature rating, which we'll cover in a moment, it's an easy way to categorise their different uses that also allows for the huge amount of individual variation between our body temperatures and how we sleep most comfortably.

- **1 season**: good for sleeping inside or warm summer nights.
- **2 season**: best for UK summers, you can always unzip it if it's a bit warm.
- **3 season**: usable most of the year but not warm enough for a frosty night.
- **4 season**: for winter nights that go below 0°C (32°F).
- **5 season**: specialist cold-weather or high-altitude sleeping bags for very cold temperatures.

In reality, no one sleeping bag is suitable for all seasons – a 4- or 5-season bag will be far too warm in summer – so choose the one that suits the majority of the camping you'll be doing and be prepared to add extra blankets or sleep with the zip open if it's unusually cold or warm. In general, a 3-season bag should be suitable for most trips.

Most sleeping bags will also have a temperature rating, indicating the temperature range they are most suitable for. All adult sleeping bags are required to be independently tested and given an ISO standard rating. This means that even given the individual variation between people, you can at least compare sleeping bags from different brands accurately. Standardised temperature ratings include a comfort rating, in which you should be comfortable all night; a lower limit range, in which you might need to sleep curled up, but you shouldn't feel uncomfortably cold; and an extreme limit, in which you're likely to be uncomfortably cold but you shouldn't actually succumb to hypothermia.

Children's sleeping bags aren't rated because of the difficulties involved in carrying out a controlled sleep experiment with children, but most children's sleeping bags will still be labelled with a season rating.

TEMPERATURE RATING

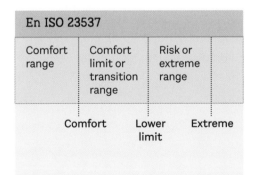

En ISO 23537		
Comfort range	Comfort limit or transition range	Risk or extreme range

Comfort   Lower limit   Extreme

For normal use, the comfort range is the best indicator of the conditions the sleeping bag will work best in. Check the average night-time temperatures in the areas you'd like to camp in the season you'd like to be able to camp and match the comfort temperature to this. If it's a bit colder than average or if you go earlier or later in the season than normal, you can always use a blanket.

If you're trying to save weight, plan to wear full base layers and a jacket to bed, and don't mind being a bit chilly, then the lower (but not the extreme) limit is a useful figure.

Female-specific sleeping bag considerations

As well as individual variation due to everything from genetics to body composition affecting how warm or cold we feel at night, males and females differ in their preference for night-time temperature. This, and differences in male and female anatomy, are why many brands make female-specific sleeping bags. These are shaped with more room at the hips and less at the shoulders and place more insulation in the core and foot areas. They also tend to be shorter so if you're a taller woman, they may not work for you. Female campers may also want to take into account the natural fluctuations in body temperature that occur throughout the menstrual cycle – you may need to factor in an extra blanket in the first half of your cycle (days 1–14 or menstruation to ovulation) when body temperature is lowest, or a lighter-weight bag in the second half (days 14–28 or ovulation to menstruation) in order to be as comfortable as possible. Menopausal campers may find lightweight cotton sheets far more comfortable than overly warm synthetic sleeping bags.

Sleeping bag fabrics

The outer and lining material used to make a sleeping bag varies from durable and breathable natural cotton to a lighter-weight, quick-drying nylon or polyester. Cotton is great when pack size and weight aren't an issue, and many people find natural fabrics more comfortable to sleep in. Additionally, cotton doesn't shed plastic

The advantage of a synthetic fill over a natural one such as down is that it will perform better in wet or damp conditions

microfibres during washing and general use in the same way that synthetic fabrics do. But synthetic fabrics are much lighter, pack smaller and dry more quickly than cotton, making these better suited to times when weight and pack size are a priority, or when the bag is likely to get wet.

The outer material of a sleeping bag is sometimes treated with a DWR (durable water repellent) coating to make it more water- and stain-resistant. In the past, most manufacturers used PFC (per- and polyfluorinated chemicals)-based DWR treatments. However, increasing evidence suggests that PFCs pollute water across the globe and bioaccumulate in the tissues of animals and humans, where they are linked to numerous potential problems with growth and reproduction, cancers, and respiratory and other illnesses. As a result, many companies are moving away from PFC-based DWR treatments and it seems wise to choose PFC-free sleeping bags, outdoor clothing and equipment.

Sleeping bags are filled with either a synthetic (usually polyester) fluff, or a

down and feather mix. Sometimes, natural wadding such as cotton or wool is used, but this is more common in lifestyle products rather than those designed for wilder environments. The fluff lofts (puffs up) to fill the space between the inner and outer material, trapping the warm air rising from the enclosed body in this space. The warmth of the sleeping bag is therefore determined by the insulating efficiency of the material and the amount of it as well as, to a certain extent, the materials sandwiching the insulation.

Synthetic fibres have a wide range of different insulation efficiencies, depending on their quality, with the best getting very close to matching down. The advantage of a synthetic fill over a natural one such as down is that it will perform better in wet or damp conditions, it's easier to wash and dry, it's generally cheaper and doesn't require the use of animal products.

Down insulation is a mixture of the downy plumage found under the feathers of geese or ducks with the addition of some of the smaller feathers. The best-quality down sleeping bags will have a ratio of about 90 per cent down to 10 per cent feather, but cheaper down sleeping bags can have a much higher feather content. A small amount of feather is extremely hard to remove and gives the down a little bit of structure to loft around, but feathers don't loft as well, so a higher percentage of feather will reduce the efficiency of the insulation – and therefore its warmth-to-weight ratio.

The quality and thermal efficiency of down is rated by its fill power or 'fluffiness'. The higher the fill power rating, the warmer the down will be for its weight. Fill power ratings range from about 450 up to 900 and very occasionally 1,000 for the highest-quality down. Measuring techniques vary slightly between the USA and Europe, but basically measure the volume that a set weight of down, processed in a prespecified way, takes up in a cylinder.

Down fill is also rated according to the weight of down used – this means for products designed to be as light as possible for their weight, a small amount of very high-quality down can be used. To achieve the same warmth with lower-quality down that has a lower fill power, a greater weight of down would be required.

These measurements and ratings are all very well in theory, but as soon as a down-filled item has been worn for a few months or packed into the bottom of a rucksack, its ability to loft will reduce. When wet, down clumps together rather than lofting and loses most of its insulating ability. Some down sleeping bags are treated to make the down more waterproof (hydrophobic down), therefore maintaining more of its insulating properties. Even so, if you expect to be camping in wet environments then a synthetic fill may suit you best. To get the best out of your down it's important to care for it properly, including meticulously drying and airing it after use. For full washing and care instructions for all your technical kit, see Chapter 6.

Unlike synthetic fills, down will naturally biodegrade at the end of its useful life. Some brands also take back used down clothing and equipment so the down fill can

▼ Fun and functional; wearable sleeping bag suits from Selk'bag

be cleaned and reused – because of the way in which it's processed, recycled down is just as high quality as new. Some down is a by-product of the meat industry, but some birds are farmed specifically for their down. If you decide to buy a down sleeping bag, look for one filled with recycled down or, if it contains new down, a Responsible Down Standard (RDS) certification. This stops the horrible practice of live plucking the birds and guarantees that they were raised in line with welfare standards.

Sleeping bag suits, such as those made by Selk'bag, are another alternative to traditional-style sleeping bags. With arms, legs and a hood, they're great for warmth and movement while sleeping as well as for ambling about camp and sitting cosily outside the tent in the evenings. Very popular with older children!

Sleeping bag liners

Whichever sleeping bag you go for, getting a sleeping bag liner to go inside it is a good idea. Available in a range of materials, they add warmth, comfort and ease of washing as well as protecting your sleeping bag and keeping it performing well for longer. Here's an overview of the various options for sleeping bag liners:

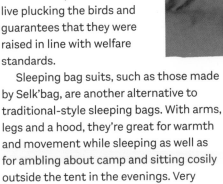

◄ An inflatable canoe or SUP can be used as a comfortable sleeping pad and saves carrying a dedicated mat

- Cotton is cool and breathable and feels comfortable against the skin, making a synthetic sleeping bag feel more like normal bedding. Cotton liners add bulk without much warmth, so they're best for summer car camping trips.
- Silk liners feel amazing against the skin, combining the natural breathability of cotton with a soft and silky feel. Silk is lightweight and packs down to a tiny size while adding a surprising amount of warmth, but it's more expensive than cotton or synthetic options. Silk production often involves highly questionable practices for both the people and creatures involved, so do your research before buying.
- Merino wool liners add a cosy, breathable, naturally anti-microbial layer between you and your sleeping bag – a little like wearing a good base layer under a technical jacket. They effectively add warmth to any sleeping bag and can also

be used on their own on warmer nights, making them very versatile. As with other animal-derived materials, check for animal welfare accreditation on products before buying.

- Fleece or microfleece polyester liners add a few degrees of warmth to a sleeping bag and the brushed fabric also feels snuggly. They're not particularly light or packable but they can be a good way of adding a few degrees of extra warmth to your sleeping bag.
- Vapour barrier liners are designed for expedition use. They stop moisture given off by the body and breath from soaking into the sleeping bag and reducing its thermal efficiency. While they do protect your expensive down sleeping bag and allow it to offer maximum warmth, they don't feel very nice.

▲ You'll find a vast choice of sleeping bags, mats and liners in your local outdoor shop

Pillows

We're the first to admit that we've yet to find anything commercially available that makes us want to leave our pillows behind when we're car camping – there's just nothing out there that can match the comfort and familiarity of a favourite pillow. But when space and weight is at a premium there are a few other options, and what one lightweight backpacker can put up with isn't necessarily what another can (or wants to) put up with.

Blow-up camping pillows give you a decent amount of depth and firmness, but they can feel and smell a bit strange. If you go down this route, take a comfortable cover – or wrap it in a Merino wool base layer or similar for a nicer feel.

Soft, compressible, microfibre-filled camping pillows feel nicer than the inflatable versions but won't offer the depth or support you'd get with a proper pillow.

For those who really don't mind, the lightest option is to use a fleece inside the stuff sack of your sleeping bag.

Camping quilts

Quilts are becoming more popular, especially with minimalist campers, as they're far less heavy and bulky than a sleeping bag but can offer a decent amount of comfort. Unlike a traditional bag, the sleeping mat provides the underbody insulation, doing away with the excess material and squashed sleeping bag insulation. Technical quilts sometimes have a single layer of fabric or flat straps under the body to hold a sleeping mat in place and reduce pesky draughts.

Pros: Quilts made from technical fabrics can be the lightest (and smallest) option for a given temperature, especially if you share a double quilt with a partner.

Cons: Not so good if you move around a lot in your sleep as you're likely to regularly let the warm air escape. Must be used with a good sleeping mat.

Camping furniture

During our year under canvas, we initially made the decision not to take camping chairs with us. We assumed we'd be fine sitting on cushions on the floor. But after a few weeks we could no longer ignore the protests of our knees, grumbling after so long spent bent or weight-bearing. While most of us spend far too much of our time sitting in chairs – whether at home, at the office or in our cars – this brief spell without them reminded us that they can, when used in moderation, be a very good thing. We still remember the joy of being able to relax into a chair and stretch out our legs again.

As well as being useful inside the tent, camping chairs are great for sociable evenings around the fire or stargazing outside the tent. Sitting on the cold floor isn't quite the same, no matter how many blankets and cushions you have.

There's a huge variety of camping chairs available to suit all budgets and requirements. In our experience, the worst ones fall over and fall apart, while the best ones are a joy to use and last for many years. We use our Helinox chairs in the garden and take them to outdoor events as well as on every camping trip – ten years after we first bought them, they're still as good as new and they definitely rank among our favourite items of camping kit.

Camping chairs generally fall into one of the following categories:

- **The classic beach deck chair** that's comfortable but takes up a lot of space. Can be cheap and cheerful but can also be very classy and well-made. Typical pack size is 60 x 70 x 120cm (24 x 28 x 48in) and 3–8kg (6lb 10oz–17lb 10oz).
- **Directors' chairs** fold flat and are comfortable although quite upright, and the pack size is still quite wide and long. Typical pack size is 60 x 10 x 70cm (24 x 4 x 28in) and 2–5kg (4lb 7oz–11lb 4oz).
- **The standard camping chair** with arms is comfortable, relaxed and often features a handy drink holder in the arm rest. Available to suit all budgets and with plenty of variation in the style and quality. The frame concertinas in on itself to create a thinner but long pack size. Typical pack size is 90 x 25 x 25cm (36 x 10 x 10in) and 2–3kg (4lb 7oz–6lb 10oz).
- **Lightweight camping chairs** use a tent-pole-type frame with fabric stretched between them. The lightweight versions tend to be at the higher end of the camping chair price range, but cheaper steel-legged versions are available that pack down to a similar size but weigh more. They are comfortable but do take a little time to assemble. They pack down the smallest and, when made with high-quality aluminium poles, can be light enough to take bikepacking, canoe/kayak camping and even backpacking. Typical pack size is 35 x 10 x 10cm (14 x 4 x 4in) and from around 500g (17.6oz).
- **Camping stools** are basic, light, small and can be cheap but still allow you to sit comfortably and off the floor. Typical pack size is 40 x 5 x 5cm (16 x 2 x 2in) and 300–500g (10.6–17.6oz).

- **Blow-up chairs** and sofas are big and comfortable and, although heavy, they don't take up much space when packed. Bring blankets and a puncture repair kit though as they can feel cold and are prone to damage. Typical pack size for a chair is 40 x 30 x 10cm (16 x 12 x 4in) and 4kg (8lb 13oz).

▼ Lightweight, packable and comfortable Helinox camping chairs

TOP
TIP

CAMPING CHAIRS

● Sitting outside the tent of an evening can quickly become chilly, so some insulation for your chairs is well worth considering. Some chairs come ready insulated; others have insulating covers available to purchase separately. Or just add your sleeping bag and/or a couple of cosy blankets and snuggle in.

● Some camping chairs have small feet that sink in soft ground the moment you sit down – a far from relaxing experience. Tiny groundsheets that fix to the feet of the chair or flat/ball-shaped foot adaptors stop this from happening, or make your own foot adaptors using cut-up tennis balls.

After chairs, a table is also very useful. It makes preparing and eating meals easier and gives you an off-the-floor space to put things. It's also much easier for younger kids to eat at a table than from a bowl or plate in their lap. Like all things camping, there's a range of options to suit all requirements. The smallest fold-up tables are useful if space is limited, but without a hard, flat surface it's difficult not to knock drinks over. Other than that – a table is a table!

Do you really need any other furniture? Browsing websites and catalogues of camping gear, or ambling around a big camping shop, it's easy to imagine you need to kit yourself out with a vast array of camping furniture, from wardrobes to kitchen cupboards, bedside storage units to laundry bins, and a whole host of clever boxes that double as seats, tables or stools. Some of these might be useful, especially if you have a big tent and you're going to be set up at the same campsite for several weeks, but don't buy them all before your first trip. Instead, go with the basics and work out if you really need anything extra as you go. After all, so much of the joy of camping lies in its stripped-back simplicity, which can easily get lost somewhere in the frenzied excitement of consumerism.

Having said all this, there are some items we have come to view as essential for our camping trips, tried-and-tested over many years. Here's our list:

- Sturdy waterproof plastic tubs with secure lids are great for storing food and other items. They are packable, prevent their contents from getting wet, scavenged by opportunistic animals or squashed during transport, and double as tables/seats – just add a tablecloth or cushion!

▶ (*Opposite*) Multitasking at Eskdale campsite

◀ A pair of fold up camping chairs

- Leave your wardrobe at home. But if you want to keep some clothes looking smart for an evening meal at a local restaurant, a dress or suit bag that can be hung up on a tent pole will keep them nicely flat and protected.
- A roomy, waterproof washbag is great for camping, allowing you to keep all your personal washing/grooming essentials in one place and easily carry them to/from the washrooms.
- A little like a washbag, a kitchen roll or chef's roll allows you to keep your knives, kitchen utensils and cutlery in one place and hangs up for easy storage and access.
- Reusable cloth shopping bags are great as laundry bags – and can be washed with your clothes.

Power

Much of the joy of camping lies in getting back to nature and living a simpler life. But we're the first to admit that sometimes going completely off-grid can create more stress than it relieves. Having to find a cafe purely to charge a phone or camera, or missing out on potential work due to the inability to check emails, have both left us frustrated in the past. Camping doesn't need to be too stripped back, especially if you're not on a super-lightweight trip. It's nice to be able to have a few comforts and power allows you to keep important items charged as well as providing simple lighting and entertainment. In this section, we'll

explore the options for bringing electrical power to your tent, both on campsites and in wilder settings.

Electric hook-up

Many campsites offer pitches with electric hook-up for a small additional charge. This allows you to plug into the campsite's electricity supply to use in your tent. You will need a camping-specific hook-up unit designed for this purpose. With some exceptions (usually older-style hook-ups), these have a round plug with round pins to plug into the campsite's power socket and then a weatherproof

socket or multiple sockets specific to that country's set-up at the other end. In the UK, these sockets fit the standard three-pin plugs, but the plug type will vary according to the country or area you're visiting. Adaptors allow you to use one unit with different campsite plugs.

Important safety note: Always use a camping-specific hook-up lead. These are designed to be used outdoors and are much safer than a standard home extension cable, plus:

- The cable is orange so shows up on grass or gravel, reducing the likelihood of it being tripped over.

- The unit will be weatherproof, and dust- and damp-resistant.
- The cable is designed to carry the current from the supply.
- The unit will have its own miniature circuit breaker to protect you and the campsite's electricity circuit.

The next section deals with understanding electric hook-up and working out how many appliances you should be able to plug into a campsite supply without causing any problems. However, if, like us, you're finding your knowledge of electrical circuits is a little hazy, here's a quick reminder, thanks to the excellent website at www. electricalsafetyfirst.org.uk, which also has a calculator you can use.

Amps

Amps measure the flow of electricity as an electric current. You should think of electric current as the flow of water through a hosepipe. The more water flowing through the hosepipe, the stronger the current is.

Volts

Volts (V) are the measurement used to determine how much force is needed to cause the electric current to flow. In keeping with the earlier example, you could think of volts as the water pressure in the hosepipe, which makes the water flow.

Watts

Amps multiplied by volts equals watts, which is the measurement used to determine the amount of energy. The higher the wattage is, the more power and output from the appliance. In terms of the hosepipe example, this would refer to the amount of water being released.

Most campsites will supply electricity

at 16 amps, but you will sometimes find 10 amp or even 5 amp supplies. It's important to know the supply rating so you don't overload the circuit and trip the supply – never a popular move on a busy campsite. If in doubt, check with campsite staff.

Your electric hook-up unit will supply this current to your equipment at 230V like at home (in Europe); other countries use different voltages (America 120V and Japan 100V).

Appliances such as kettles, toasters and hairdryers are usually rated in kilowatts (kW), each of which is 1,000 watts, telling you how much energy that appliance requires to run. It's important that the sum total of everything you have plugged in doesn't exceed the maximum available from the supply.

Using the equation below, you can work out the total kW you can use at the campsite and divide this between your

▼ A typical campsite electric hook-up

appliances so you know how many, and which type, you can plug in at a time:

amps × volts = watts

CALCULATING KW ACCORDING TO VOLTAGE

Europe and 230V countries	North America and 120V countries
230V × 16 amp supply = 3,680W or 3.68kW	120V × 16 amp supply = 19,200W or 1.92kW
230V × 10 amp supply = 2,300W or 2.3kW	120V × 10 amp supply = 1,200W or 1.2kW
230V × 5 amp supply = 1,150W or 1.15kW	120V × 5 amp supply = 600W or 0.6kW

The table (right) lists normal power ratings for some common electrical devices. Devices will vary but this will give you a good idea of what to expect. As you can see, charging phones and other devices doesn't use much power, but heating devices such as hairdryers and heaters usually use a lot. The table also demonstrates the benefit of using a camping-specific kettle.

NORMAL POWER RATINGS FOR DEVICES

Device	Power (watts)
Smartphone charging	5 (0.005kW)
Laptop charging	60 (0.06kW)
Camping lights	10 (0.01kW)
Electric heater on low power	1,000 (1kW)
Electric heater on full power	2,000 (2kW)
Kettle from home	2,000 (2kW)
Camping kettle	750 (0.75kW)
Hairdryer on lowest setting	100 (0.1kW)
Hairdryer on full power	800 (0.8kW)

If you do accidentally trip the switch, most campsite hook-up units have a mini circuit breaker, so you'll only turn your own gadgets off. To reset this, make sure that you've turned off the high-power devices and then flick the circuit breaker switch on the hook-up and plug back to on. Occasionally – and we've done this once – it's possible to trip the switch for the entire campsite, at which point you'll need to apologise unreservedly to your neighbours and find a member of staff to turn it all back on again.

> It's possible to trip the switch for the entire campsite, at which point you'll need to apologise unreservedly to your neighbours and find a member of staff to turn it all back on again.

Power banks

Available in a range of capacities and power outputs, from small units that can recharge a smartphone to larger and more powerful units capable of powering a kettle or supplying off-grid power for a couple of days, power banks are simply rechargeable batteries with circuitry built in that allows you to plug in a range of devices in order to utilise the battery's power. They're really handy to take camping for recharging devices such as phones, cameras and laptops, or even powering a camping kettle. Basic small units normally just have a USB output, but the more powerful (and expensive) power banks will have a range of outlets including all the different-style USB sockets, 12V DC (car cigarette lighter-style) socket and 240V AC three-pin plugs (or regional equivalent).

The battery size or capacity of a power bank is measured in watt hours (Wh). This means that, starting fully charged, a 30Wh power bank could power a 30W device (or three 10W devices) for one hour. Power banks are available from around 30Wh up to at least 2,000Wh to suit your needs.

The maximum power of the unit will be given in watts (W). To work out the maximum power you'll need, add up the watts ratings of the devices you'll want to power at the same time; the power bank must offer a watts rating higher than this maximum. You can check the table of

▼ Lightweight power banks are a convenient and portable way to charge electronics in remote areas

normal power ratings for devices in the table on page 96.

Once your power bank has run out of power, it'll need recharging. Most smaller power banks recharge using a USB C, while larger devices run off 12V and 240V wall plug inputs. Many can also be connected to solar panels to provide an off-grid charge source during daylight hours.

Leisure battery and inverter

This set-up is similar to that found in a campervan or caravan. When using this system as your sole source of power, it can last several days between charges with careful use.

A leisure battery looks like a car battery, but it's designed to run without charge for

longer, supplying a lower peak power and coping with a deeper drain and recharge cycle. A leisure battery will provide 12V power like a car's cigarette lighter socket. You can set the battery up to provide a socket to charge phones and run camping appliances such as cool boxes that are designed to run off a 12V socket. In general, bigger and heavier (and more expensive) batteries will provide more charging time between recharges. Batteries are rated in amp hours (Ahrs), or the total amount of current (amps) it can supply for one hour.

An inverter steps up the 12V DC supply from the leisure battery and allows you

▼ Using a leisure battery and inverter means you can run more powerful electronic items as you would at home

TYPICAL USAGE AND BATTERY LIFE FOR DIFFERENT INVERTERS

	Usage	Leisure battery life (100 Ahr battery)
150W inverter	Charging batteries, phones, camera etc.	75W usage = 14 hours
300W inverter	Charging devices and running lighting	150W usage = 6.5 hours
500W inverter	Also powering camping devices like kettle, TV, low-power hair dryer etc.	250W usage = 4 hours
2,000W inverter	More power available	1,000W usage = 1 hour

to run 230V AC devices as you would at home. Inverters are available with different maximum power capacities to suit your required usage. Lower power ratings will be cheaper initially, and the battery will last for longer, but you may be limited in what you can power. You can buy 1,000W and even 2,000W inverters but when used off-grid with a leisure battery they have the potential to drain the battery in an hour or less, so they don't tend to be a great idea for camping.

The table above shows typical usage and battery life for different inverters. For the comparison, I've used half the maximum W draw available from the inverter and a 100 Ahr battery. The temperature and the age or condition of the battery will affect its maximum Ahrs so in real use you wouldn't expect to reach the maximum run time quoted.

To work out your own usage for your system, first use this formula:

= amps drawn from the battery

Then:

= Battery life in hours

Campervans and caravans are likely to be set up to recharge the battery when driving, as well as when connected to an external power source such as a campsite hook-up. If you're using a leisure battery without electric hook-up, you can use solar panels to charge the battery during daylight hours.

Solar charging

If you don't have electric hook-up and you're planning on being away for more than a couple of days, then you need a way to charge your phone, power bank or leisure battery system that you use. Solar charging is the easiest and best way to do this. Solar panels can charge devices directly or plug into power banks or batteries to save the charge for when you need it. They generate the most electricity in bright sunlight, but they will produce electricity on cloudy days, too, so they should work all year round. In all cases, solar panels need to be clean to be most effective. They will also work much better in direct sunlight rather than behind a car or tent window, so keep them outside if possible. The panels are available in a variety of designs and sizes to match your needs. Some are also waterproof, which means you don't need to worry about leaving them charging when you're not at the camp.

Some solar panels come with an internal battery that can be used in the same way as a power bank, others only charge devices directly. Check that the panel you decide to buy has the connections that you need.

Larger panels produce more power, but solar panels are available in three main forms and the efficiency varies:

▼ Lightweight and portable solar panels allow you to work from anywhere sunny

1 Monocrystalline panels are the most efficient but also the most expensive. They have a rigid construction and the glass covering is fragile. They produce the best power output in low light conditions.
2 Polycrystalline panels are slightly less efficient but cheaper. They have a rigid construction, and the glass covering is fragile.
3 Amorphous silicon panels are less efficient again but they can be flexible so you can roll up the panels when not in use. They are lighter and more durable so are good for backpacking.

The panel's power rating will determine what type of device it can charge directly and how quickly it will charge, usually rated as watts per hour. A 5W panel will charge a phone, 10W to 30W will charge cameras and laptops, and you'll need around 100W

▲ BioLite solar panels charging a lantern and iPad

to power a cool box. Any power rating can be used to add charge to a power bank or leisure battery, but lower-power panels will charge more slowly and may not fully recharge the unit over the course of a day. The actual output of the panel is affected by the strength of the sunlight, so you won't always get the full power that the panel can theoretically produce. If you need more power, some solar panels can be linked together – this is often known as chaining.

Generators

In some circumstances, bringing a portable diesel or petrol generator may be appropriate and will provide you with all the power you need. However, you are not normally allowed to use generators on commercial campsites.

Lighting

Sitting outside the tent after supper on a warm, clear evening, watching the stars come out, spotting bats and maybe an owl or a fox is one of our favourite camping pastimes. Campsites are often further away from sources of light pollution, resulting in far darker skies and giving us the ability to see many more stars and planets than we can at home.

This is all great until you need to find something in the dark tent, or you trip over a guy line on the way to the sinks with your arms piled high with washing-up. Happily, lighting in and around your tent is easy to arrange with or without electric hook-up. Modern LED lighting requires very little power, so battery torches and lanterns can last a few days between charges. It's also quite likely that you already have some lights that would be suitable at home. Children love having a torch of their own and gifting them one helps get them ready for camping adventures.

Depending on your style of camping, you can be minimalist and weight conscious with lighting, relying on a single head torch to provide all the light you need, or you can go for the comfort and convenience of lanterns and fairy lights to light the camp, with torches at the ready for any forays away from the camp.

Most torches have an output measured in lumens. The higher the number, the brighter the light. Lanterns don't always give a lumen figure but as they're generally used to provide a diffuse light, this isn't a problem. The lumen number is most important for a hand-held or head torch with which you want to be able to shine the light a long distance. The beam pattern will also affect the light output: a narrow beam reaches further but won't illuminate the areas to either side. A more dispersed or floodlight beam will offer a wider field of view without shadowy areas to the sides but won't reach as far. Some torches have an adjustable beam so that you get both options. For camping, a wider beam is normally more useful and lower-power torches or at least a torch with a lower power option is generally better unless you want to spotlight the whole campsite.

Electric lanterns

Super-useful and worth packing in all but the most weight conscious of situations, electric lanterns range from small and lightweight, perfect for backpacking, all the way through to large units to light a group gathering or event. Lanterns produce a diffuse cloud of light that's ideal for illuminating an area like a tent porch or picnic table. More powerful lanterns (higher lumens) will provide brighter light and illuminate a bigger area, but the full-power mode could be too bright in a small space so look for those with low-power modes. Some models feature softer or even coloured light settings so you can create a nice, relaxed feel in the evenings. It's handy to be able to hang a lantern up, so look for an easy-to-use clip or handle.

Most electric lanterns are battery powered – and many are rechargeable. Check that the time between charges suits what you'll be using it for. For those that run off replaceable batteries, these can also be

rechargeable, and this also means you can have a spare set available. Some lanterns double as a power bank, so you can charge a phone from them via a USB connection. This can be a useful feature but does drain the battery faster.

One of the best we've found for general car camping is a small, rechargeable lantern from BioLite. As well as bright white and soft white settings, it has different colour modes and even one that flickers like a candle. The lowest setting works well as a nightlight, while on full power it lights the tent sufficiently to work or eat supper. It also has a USB output for charging a phone, plus a hanging loop. For a lighter-weight option, turn your head torch into a handy lantern using a converter such as the Petzl Noctilight. This houses a small head torch and diffuses the light, so it acts as a lantern – it also has a hanging clip.

Gas and liquid fuel lanterns

These lanterns give out a nice, even area of light and come in a range of sizes to suit most needs. The light is a bit softer and less insistent than an electric light, and they don't rely on having power available for recharging so, although they're less convenient than a simple on/off battery lantern, they're well worth considering. Gas and liquid fuel lanterns also give off some heat, which can be welcome on a cold evening.

Liquid fuel lanterns work on a pressurised system whereby the fuel is heated and compressed until it becomes a gas, so they burn exactly like a gas lantern. The gas is released into a mantle where it's burned, and this gives off light and heat. You can increase the brightness by allowing more gas into the mantle, so the burn is more intense.

Most gas lanterns use a toughened glass surround, which is both heatproof and windproof, but this does make them more fragile. The mantle looks like a string bag when new but once installed and used it becomes brittle, so this can also be easily damaged. It's always worth carrying a spare mantle anyway – they only weigh a few grams.

Gas and liquid fuel lanterns should be used in a well-ventilated area and not inside a tent.

Candles and candle lanterns

A few candles in jars or candle holders provide a gentle, atmospheric light but they're a fire risk and tend to blow out easily. For the same feel with better safety, candle lanterns house one or more candles inside a glass and metal housing. This means that you can move them around and hang them up, and they're windproof and much safer, although they still get hot. Like gas lanterns, they give off a nice atmospheric light and, especially for those that take several candles, even a little heat. Citronella candles are available that work with camping candle lanterns, which may help keep biting insects away.

Candles should be used in a well-ventilated area and not inside an enclosed tent.

Hurricane lanterns

These design classics burn lamp oil or a different petroleum-based liquid from a wick. They are almost completely wind- and rainproof once lit and provide a very nice but not hugely bright light. In the base of the lantern is a fuel tank: a fabric wick hangs into this and soaks up the fuel. You light the wick in the burner and replace the weatherproof glass bulb. The wick will continue to soak up and burn the fuel until it runs out.

Hurricane lamps should be used in a well-ventilated area and not inside a tent.

Head torches

With a powerful, focused light and hands-free use, head torches are great for camping, as well as general after-dark adventures. We use ours for everything from pitching the tent when we've arrived late on a campsite to washing-up. They're great for children, too, enabling them (and us!) to see where they're going. As mentioned above, a head torch can even be transformed into a handy hanging lantern by using a light-diffusing case such as the Petzl Noctilight.

Basic head torches are affordable and give out enough light for wandering around a campsite, reading in a tent or washing-up. More high-tech (and therefore expensive) models can provide a seriously bright and long-reaching beam good enough for fast running or navigating in tough terrain in darkness. Lights are also available that can be switched between bike, head and helmet use – these tend to be costly, but they are extremely effective and versatile, an ideal choice for multi-activity use.

Head torch brightness is measured in lumens, but the length of the beam and the spread of light is also affected by the beam pattern. A more focused light gives a long, narrow beam whereas a wider beam provides a more diffuse cloud of light over a shorter distance. Most good models include the ability to vary your beam – some with responsive lighting modes do so automatically. These come with smartphone-based apps that enable you to customise your settings and keep an eye on battery use in between charges.

TYPICAL HEAD TORCH OUTPUTS IN LUMENS, BEAM LENGTH AND BEST USE

Lumen rating	Typical beam length	Best suited for
Less than 40	<20m (65ft)	Younger children and in the tent
40–150	35m (115ft)	General camping use
150–400	55m (180ft)	Walking
Greater than 400	>80m (262ft)	Running and navigation in rough terrain

Head torches are powered by rechargeable or standard batteries and some models can use both. Sometimes the battery and light are the same unit and sometimes the battery is in a separate pack mounted on the back of the head to even up the weight. Most have a comfortable and adjustable elasticated head strap that can often also be used to hang them or attach them to something as a lantern.

Hand torches

Hand torches work in the same way as head torches, but you carry them instead of wearing them on your head. This can be more useful, and a hand torch is a useful thing to have for a quick walk over to the facilities block.

TOP TIP

HEAD TORCH OR HAND TORCH?

You can always carry a head torch, so if you're only buying one torch, get a head torch.

Heating

If you're camping in the colder months, a small heater can be a great thing. Waking up on a freezing morning or getting back to a cold tent after a long day in the hills and turning on a heater for a quick blast of hot air always makes everything feel better. Tents tend to warm up rapidly while the heater is on but cool down even faster once it's switched off again.

Fire is a real concern in a tent so always use the heating units as they are intended.

Don't hang items to dry directly on heaters and take care they don't get covered by a stray sleeping bag if you're leaving one on overnight. Be very wary of carbon monoxide poisoning if you have a wood burner inside a tent and definitely don't mix using fire and synthetic tent materials.

Depending on your tent material, the amount of weight you can carry, your location and the power sources available here are the main heating options.

Electric heating

If you have electric hook-up or a powerful off-grid system, a small electric heater is probably the safest and most convenient option. Just check the power required doesn't exceed that available from your source (see the table on page 96).

Fan or convection heaters give off heat almost instantly, which is really useful for warming up the tent quickly and cleanly. Convection heaters and oil-filled radiators are also quiet, so they can be left on overnight if it's very cold, but this will drain a battery fast so plenty of warm clothing and a good, well-insulated sleeping system is far more efficient.

Infrared heaters are a good choice for outdoor or well-ventilated settings that are difficult and/or inefficient to heat through other means. Infrared light isn't visible because it's beyond the spectrum that human eyes are able to see. The heat produced by infrared is a product of this invisible light, which is absorbed by our skin and clothes. Warmth is only felt from an infrared source if you're directly within its range – like the feeling of heat from the sun that disappears as soon as you enter shade. The sun is still there, but its radiant heat isn't reaching you as well.

Gas heaters

Gas heaters run off small disposable gas cylinders or larger refillable cylinders. They give off a good amount of heat and warm up quickly. Due to the risk of carbon monoxide poisoning, gas heating shouldn't be used inside a tent or other enclosed space. They are good for warming your feet of an evening and work well under a tarp if there is plenty of air circulation. We would always recommend a carbon monoxide alarm for your tent if you're using gas heating nearby.

▼ Outwell Katla Camping Heater

Wood burners

Wood burning stoves designed specifically for outdoor and camping use can be installed in cotton tents like tipis or bell tents. They shouldn't be used in nylon or polyester tents as any sparks will melt holes in the tent, but cotton is fireproof enough to cope with the occasional spark. We used a Frontier wood burning stove for a few months over the winter in a canvas bell tent and found it invaluable as a source of cooking, heating and hot water, which was on constant resupply from a handy tank that wrapped around the flue.

The flue from a wood burner exits the tent through a weather- and heatproof

▶ Anevay Frontier™ portable wood burning stove

▼ Tentipi Zirkon 7 Light and Eldfell Stove in Sweden, photographer Karl & Moa Gräsmark

flashing, known as a stove jack in the USA. This consists of two metal rings that are fastened together on either side of a hole cut in the canvas, and a silicone sleeve through which the flue runs from the inside to the outside. The flue acts as a chimney, drawing smoke and gases from the inside of the burner straight into the outside air, rather than into your tent.

Spark arresters are mesh sleeves that sit at the top of the flue – sometimes these are integrated but otherwise you'll need to buy one separately. These allow smoke to escape but trap any sparks or burning fragments, so they don't damage or ignite your tent or other equipment. A fireproof mat positioned under your wood burner will protect both the groundsheet and the earth underneath.

When using a wood burner, make sure that the tent is ventilated and always use a CO alarm in the tent. We also keep a fire blanket and fire extinguisher nearby, attached to a tent pole, just in case.

Once safely set up and burning well, a wood burner gives off a good amount of heat and provides a flat hotplate for cooking on. Always use completely dry wood to avoid smoking out the tent, or alternatively use compressed fire logs, which burn well but are more expensive. We'll often have a few of these for those times when we need to get the fire going quickly but use whole wood the majority of the time.

While they work well and feel wonderfully self-sufficient to use, the downside of a wood burner is the time it takes to clean – including regularly cleaning the flue to avoid build-up of residue, which could cause

TOP TIP

KEEPING YOUR WOOD DRY

Storing your kindling and wood near to the wood burner helps to keep it dry during camping trips.

a blockage – along with getting it burning well in the first place. If a wood burner is your sole source of heat, the first person up each day has the unenviable and cold task of lighting it, but the effort is heartily rewarded with a cosy tent and hot porridge bubbling away by the time everyone else is up. Breakfast on a crisp autumn morning around the wood burner is a lovely thing.

Fire

Fire and tents don't work well in close proximity, so open fires are best reserved for sleeping out. Using a canvas bedroll or canvas bivi bag is safer than a synthetic alternative when there's the risk of stray sparks flying around. If you do decide an open fire is appropriate, set a shift pattern so that someone is awake to keep it burning and safe.

Hot water bottles

In cold weather, taking a hot water bottle to bed helps warm up your sleeping bag quickly. In freezing conditions, pouring hot water into a drinking bottle with a secure lid and wrapping it in a protective covering acts as a hot water bottle. By the morning you'll have cold but not frozen water to drink, too.

Electric blankets

Electric blankets aren't really intended for camping. The travel versions that are designed to run off rechargeable batteries or a 12V car socket can be good for snuggling up in the evening, but they're not safe for tent sleeping. Electric blankets and moisture aren't a good mix and in a tent it's very hard to completely avoid condensation, water brought in with wet clothing, or spills. Electric blankets shouldn't be used over a sleeping bag as they can overheat and it's possible to melt the synthetic outer material of a sleeping bag. If you do decide to use one, then it's best to get one with a safety feature to automatically turn off if it starts to overheat and to make sure you turn it off before you go to sleep.

Water

Most, but by no means all, campsites will provide drinking water for campers. Many will be connected to the local mains water system, so if mains water is safe to drink then the campsite water should be fine. Tap water is safe in almost all of western Europe, North America, New Zealand and Japan as well as many other countries worldwide, but always check before you go.

Depending on the facilities and size of the campsite, you'll find drinking water taps at the wash block and around the site. To save multiple journeys to the tap, a large water carrier with a tap can be useful. Rolling water carriers with a handle make the journey back from the tap easier.

Wilderness camping adventures can take us to many places where the quality of the water is unknown, from streams,

◄▲ Using a LifeStraw Flex filter bottle to collect and drink water while on the go

rivers and lakes to places where even the tap water should be treated with suspicion. If you're somewhere far from possible pollutants you might get away with drinking it straight from the source, but it's not generally recommended, especially as the consequences of falling ill somewhere remote and far from medical care could be serious. Consuming contaminated water can lead to unpleasant – and even life-threatening – illnesses, but the look, smell and taste of water aren't reliable indicators of what it might contain. As there's currently no easy way to test it, treating water is the best way to be sure it's safe to drink.

The pathogens found in untreated water can be broadly divided into the following groups: bacteria such as *E. coli*; viruses including hepatitis A; protozoa such as *Giardia* and *Cryptosporidium* (also sometimes called 'protozoan cysts' or simply 'cysts', as this is the stage of the protozoan's life cycle found in water); along with chemicals, metals and other substances that have the potential to cause harm if ingested.

The best treatment method depends on the source and the amount of water required. Turbid – muddy, sandy or cloudy – water will need filtering before treatment, and if you're sourcing water for a group, you'll need to use a different method to that required for just one or two people. Here's our guide to the various methods of hygienic hydration.

Wilderness camping adventures can take us to many places where the quality of the water is unknown, from streams, rivers and lakes to places where even the tap water should be treated with suspicion.

HYGIENIC HYDRATION

Boiling

According to World Health Organization guidelines, bringing water to a rolling boil for one minute – or three minutes if you're above 1,000m (3,280ft) as altitude reduces the temperature at which water will boil – is sufficient to kill off bacteria, viruses and protozoa. Although it is an effective, simple and chemical-free method, boiling all of your water is fuel- and time-consuming so, if you will be boiling all your drinking water, it's important to consider the most effective and efficient way of doing so. Stoves vary greatly in their efficiency, and some are far better designed for simply boiling water than others. Have a read of Chapter 4 to find the one that best suits your needs.

UV light

As with boiling, treating water with UV light kills off 99.9 per cent of bacteria, viruses and protozoa, but without the need to carry a stove and pan or use up camping fuel. Many UV treatment devices, like the Steripen, are small, lightweight and very convenient, and last for many uses on a single battery. Ideal for treating potentially unsafe tap water or taking into the mountains to use on water from rivers and streams, they don't filter out debris or work in cloudy water so you may need to use a filter as well.

Chemical treatments

Chlorine- and iodine-based water treatments come in cheap, portable droplet or tablet form and are highly effective at killing off many common water contaminants. Chlorine is ineffective against some strains of *Cryptosporidium* and neither treatment will remove sediment, so filtration before treatment may be required. Iodine is not suitable for pregnant women or those with thyroid disorders.

Filtration

Water filters physically remove particles so they're ideal for cloudy, muddy and sandy water. Pathogens and debris in water come in many shapes and sizes and manufacturers usually specify a diameter, in micrometres (millionths of a metre and also often called microns), down to which the filter is effective. Most bacteria have a diameter of 1–10 micrometres, while the waterborne cysts of the protozoa *Giardia* and *Cryptosporidium* are 4–14 micrometres. Viruses can be as small as 20 nanometres, or 0.02 micrometres in diameter.

Filters range from pocket-sized versions that allow you to drink straight from a water source to those suitable for large groups. Microfilters remove protozoan cysts and bacteria, so further treatment with chemical or UV may be required, while purifiers, such as the LifeSaver Liberty, also remove viruses. As filters trap pathogens and debris, they need to be kept clean to maintain a good flow rate and the filters must be replaced after the recommended number of uses.

▶ Boiling water for a morning coffee using an Optimus Crux stove and a Vargo Ti pan

Washing

Campsites usually have a wash block with toilets, showers and washing-up sinks in the same place. This is often also where you will find things like waste and recycling facilities, grey water and chemical disposal, and drinking water, although many sites also have drinking water taps closer to the pitches.

A hot shower after a long day's adventures feels great and campsite showers are no longer as scary as they once were – many, in fact, could rival those in a hotel. Fortunately, it's now pretty rare to find a draughty concrete shed with a trickle of lukewarm water. If there aren't washing facilities and you're keen to stay clean, take two large bowls along – one for soapy water and one for clean – and heat some water in a pan for washing. Foldable baths are great if you're camping with young children, enabling a splash-about in the warmth and privacy of the tent.

Doing the dishes can be a communal affair in many campsites. We've enjoyed many conversations with other campers while washing-up, sharing recommendations for things to do or places to go. If you're wild camping, then the warm water and convenience of the campsite is replaced with amazing views and a secluded wash spot – it might be freezing but wow does it feel good!

Dryrobes and other similar changing robes designed for surfing and wild swimming also work really well for camping, from throwing on after a shower to cosy evening wear around the campfire.

Soaps

Soap and other chemicals used while camping can be damaging to local wildlife and pollute water sources. Campsite grey water systems should be connected to the mains sewerage system, but in remote areas this isn't always the case. Biodegradable soaps are a good idea as they won't disrupt or contaminate the ecosystem as much as conventional soaps or shampoos, but they're far from perfect so use sparingly. All-purpose biodegradable soap liquids or soap bars and leaves are available from outdoor shops, or pure castile soaps come in liquid or bar form and can be used to wash yourself, your hair, laundry, the dishes and anything else that needs to be cleaner. If you're camping in bear country, it's recommended that you choose the unscented version. If you're wild camping and want to use a soap, do so at least 50m (164ft) from any water course and make sure it's biodegradable.

Solar showers

If you're planning to use campsites without facilities or want to set up camp in a longer-term, off-grid space, there are still shower options that don't just involve a bucket of water tipped over your head. Solar showers can be made or bought and are highly effective in warm, sunny weather.

A solar shower is basically a large black water bag with a strap with which to hang it at the top. At the base of the bag is a shower-head-style nozzle that can be opened or closed. Fill the bag with cold water in the morning and leave it in direct sunshine during the day. By the evening, the sun will have warmed the water ready for a comfortable shower.

Solar showers can be hung from branches, vehicles or any other convenient hanging place. If privacy's an issue, set up a strategically placed tarp or windbreak,

◀ (*Opposite top*) Guy lines can work well as washing lines

▶ Using a Ortlieb solar shower

or you can buy small cubicle size shower tents, but these definitely detract from the pure joy of a wild shower. If you do go for a shower tent, make sure the top support is strong enough to support a heavy bag full of water, that there's somewhere to provide a hanging point, and avoid sewn-in groundsheets!

Baby baths

Collapsible baby baths or a large builder's-style flexi bucket can make washing a small child (or dog) easier and more fun. You need a good source of warm water so it may be easier to bring the bath over to the wash block unless you have some sort of water heater in the tent.

Travel towels

Packable microfibre trek towels save a huge amount of space and weight compared to standard cotton versions. Made from polyester with a looped or brushed finish, they're not as absorbent as usual towels but will dry you off effectively and will then

dry much more quickly themselves. Trek towels are available in a range of sizes from face cloth through to beach towel and also as a wearable changing robe. Travel towels are a must for backpacking or any trip where space and weight are important.

Having said all this, for summer car-camping trips we'll often take standard cotton towels as they're much nicer to use and dry quickly enough spread out in the warm sunshine. Cotton towels are also much more durable, can be hot-washed if they start to smell unsavoury, and don't shed microplastics or create plastic waste at the end of their usable life like their synthetic counterparts do.

If you're camping with a dog, it's well worth packing a few towels specifically for their use, especially if you're somewhere where they're likely to get wet and/or muddy.

Dishwashing

If space allows, a washing-up bowl makes dishwashing at a campsite much easier. Doubling as a means of transporting your dirty dishes over to the washing-up sinks, it then requires less water to fill and gives you a rinsing and draining area separate from your washing-up one. Foldable or collapsible washing-up bowls are also available and help to save space. It's best to use a biodegradable soap unless you're sure the campsite is connected to mains sewerage.

Laundry

Many campsites have a washing machine available to use for a small fee so, if you think you might need to do a wash, remember your laundry liquid or use a multipurpose biodegradable camping soap. Otherwise, you'll need to find a launderette or wash anything that really needs it by hand in the sink. Some campsites offer tumble driers, which can be useful for drying clothes on a wet trip – but don't tumble-dry your technical kit as synthetics may melt and wool might shrink. Some campsites, especially those in particularly outdoorsy places, have large, heated drying rooms where wet clothing, footwear and equipment can be hung or laid out to dry. A camping clothesline is invaluable and can be bought or easily made from several strings of elasticated cord. Hang the line between two fixed points and simply thread the clothes between the strings instead of using pegs.

Camping with dogs

Our dog loves camping trips and all the exciting new sounds, sights, smells and adventures they bring. He's usually a joy to camp with but, especially in the early days, the huge differences between camping and being at home took some getting used to. Understanding how to keep your dog happy is key to everyone having a good time.

▼ A dog-friendly campsite amongst the vineyards in Champagne

Many campsites accept dogs, but some don't, so it's well worth checking in advance if you're planning to take one along. If you're camping with a dog, it should always be kept on the lead, exercised well away from living/playing spaces, and meticulously cleaned up after. Barking, jumping up and visits to other people's tents are a definite no – bear in mind that dog people love dogs, but non-dog people often *really* don't like dogs, sometimes as a result of bad

experiences in the past, so never assume everyone feels the same way about your pooch as you do. In a campsite with plenty of space, taking a longer section of rope allows a dog to have a little more freedom near to the tent without being able to wander off.

As with all other food, keeping dog food in sealed containers is important to avoid attracting unwelcome creatures. Collapsible silicone food and water bowls are a great invention for when space is tight. Dogs can get cold at night so take a section of insulating camping mat and an extra blanket with you in cool weather, unless you don't mind them trying to join you in your sleeping bag... Expect your dog to be on the alert when you're camping, especially on the first night when all the surrounding sounds and smells are unfamiliar. We find ours settles down after a restless first night and then sleeps well in the tent – a lot like the kids.

▲ Scout out camping

Insects and unwelcome wildlife

Camping is great for getting us all closer to nature, affording encounters with animals that simply don't happen when we're cocooned in our houses. But not all creatures are welcome in our tents. Biting insects can ruin an evening, and itchy bites can wreck a whole trip. In some countries or areas, insects carry diseases so it's even more important not to get bitten. Then there are larger animals, which will normally give campers a wide berth but if hungry may take the opportunity to grab an easy-to-reach snack or could be inherently dangerous, such as marauding elephants or hippos in Africa.

There are several lines of defence to stop wild animals and insects becoming too much of a problem. The first is to keep a tidy camp, never leave food or waste uncovered, and make sure that food and anything that could

SIM: 'Sleeping peacefully in a campsite in Fontainebleau, I was woken by the loud noise of something massive rummaging in the porch of our tent. It turned out it was a badger trying to steal our croissants but, from the depths of sleep, I was convinced there must be bears in France!'

smell appealing is packed away in sealed containers. This should deter scavenging animals from mice to bears, although the strength of the containers may need to be different!

Try to site your camp well away from insect hotspots. Most airborne biting insects like warm, wet and sheltered areas, so if you can camp in an exposed place that isn't very close to a water source you won't get as many insects in the first place. Ticks like long, damp grass, especially if it's close to woodland.

Barriers

If insects can't get to you due to a physical barrier, then they can't bite you and shouldn't be a problem. One of the simplest deterrents is to wear long trousers tucked into socks, long-sleeved tops and a hat with a mosquito net attached; if they can't get to your skin, they can't bite you.

Most biting insects are attracted to the smell of humans or the carbon dioxide we breathe out. They also favour still air and humid conditions – just like those in your tent.

It's good practice to shake off clothing before you enter a tent and open the entrance flap for the shortest possible time to minimise the possibility of allowing unwanted guests in. Bugs will also find their way through the gap at the bottom of a zip and any holes in the tent, so if you're going somewhere buggy, it's worth checking your tent and making sure any inviting small holes are repaired.

The inner sleeping compartments of most tents are quite well sealed from bugs and animals, as long as you keep the zips closed. Most have insect netting as ventilation so airflow can be maintained without letting insects in. This offers great protection against mosquito-sized insects, spiders and small animals but most mesh will still allow midges, sandflies and other tiny insects through. Some tents use no-see-um mesh, or sandfly/midge-proof netting, which is finer and therefore stops all insects.

In super-lightweight bivi tents, bell tents and tipis, which may not come with an inner tent or sewn-in groundsheet, there are a few options to create an insect-free sleeping compartment. Some brands make an optional inner tent with a sewn-in groundsheet available to buy separately. Otherwise, a hanging mosquito net inside the tent creates a protected sleeping area. Lifesystems makes a range of different sizes of mosquito net, including free-standing versions that work well under a tarp.

Some insect netting is treated with an insect repellent or insecticide to stop or dissuade insects even landing on the net. This has pros and cons that we'll discuss in the next two sections.

Insect repellent

Repellents ward off insects by masking the scents that attract them or producing other scents that they don't like. They won't normally harm the insects, so repellents combined with clothing and physical barriers are the least damaging approach.

If you have a fire, such as a fire pit or wood-fired outdoor stove, this will help to keep most animals and insects away. It's said that you can increase the insect repellent qualities of smoke by adding a bunch of dried sage – in practice it's hard to know how effective this is, but it adds a nice hint of herby fragrance to the evening.

If you can't or don't want to have a fire, citronella candles may add some insect protection through a combination of smoke and scent. If it's windy then a UCO candle lantern fitted with citronella candles will burn happily, providing a warm glow with the benefit of discouraging flying insects. As stressed before, avoid using candles in an enclosed tent, but if you do decide to use one in the porch, make sure the entrance flap is open and the tent is well ventilated. Some other essential oils such as eucalyptus, lavender, peppermint and geranium are supposed to repel insects and can be used as oil or burned in candles to repel insects. Findings from a 2019 study published in the journal *Experimental and Applied Acarology* suggest that '5% oregano and spearmint oils exhibit potential as natural clothing repellents, with an effective equivalence to 20% DEET'. The same researchers found that a turmeric oil suspension was effective at preventing ticks from attaching to dogs. Clearly there's a lot more research to be done, but some promising results are emerging for natural insect repellents.

Repellents for topical application

DEET (N,N-Diethyl-meta-toluamide, or diethyltoluamide) is the most common active ingredient in insect repellents. Intended to be applied to the skin or to clothing, it provides protection against mosquitoes and many other flying insects, ticks, fleas, harvest mites (chiggers) and leeches. When using DEET-based repellents, only spray it on exposed skin like your wrists and ankles. If you want to apply it to your face, spray it on your hand and rub it on your face avoiding your mouth and eyes. It's best to apply DEET outside to avoid breathing it in.

DEET is a synthetic repellent available in different strengths measured as a percentage concentration, usually between 5 per cent and 50 per cent. The strength determines how long it will be effective for before requiring reapplication: 5 per cent DEET offers about an hour's protection while 50 per cent lasts about eight hours. A larger volume of 5 per cent DEET doesn't give you a longer protection time, nor does a smaller volume of 50 per cent give less protection, so always apply as directed and reapply when necessary. Try to match the percentage concentration to the amount of time you are likely to need protection.

PMD (p-Menthane-3,8-diol, also known as para-menthane-3,8-diol or menthoglycol) is marketed as a more 'natural' active ingredient that is also proven to repel biting insects. Often, although not always, derived from the oil of the lemon eucalyptus (*Eucalyptus citriodora*), PMD has been found to be as effective at repelling flying insects as DEET, but it needs to be at a concentration of at least 30 per cent and requires more frequent application.

IR3535 (ethyl butylacetylaminopropionate or EBAAP) is a synthetic repellent that should be used at a concentration of 20 per cent and only in places that are free from malaria. It gives complete protection comparable to DEET against several, but not all, mosquito species.

Icaridin (hydroxyethyl isobutyl piperidine carboxylate; also known as picaridin, Bayrepel and Saltidin) is a synthetic repellent that offers complete protection for up to six hours against *Anopheles*, *Aedes* and *Culex* mosquito species when used at concentrations greater than 20 per cent.

Some sun creams contain an insect repellent within them to offer insect and sun protection. It's best not to combine

▶ Applying insect repellent during a hike

the two, but instead reapply both sun cream and insect repellent when necessary. The reapplication times are likely to be different.

Insecticides

These chemicals are designed to kill the insects that they come into contact with. This could be as a vapour in the air surrounding the dispenser or when they touch the insecticide by landing on a treated surface. The problem is that they're indiscriminate and may also harm unintended insects such as bees and butterflies. Biting insects are usually worst in the early morning or late evening when bees and other positive insects are less active, so using insecticides at these times may cause less collateral damage, but it's hard to know. Limit your use of these products to when there is a high risk of insect-borne disease and high levels of biting insects.

Insecticides are usually distributed by heating or burning an impregnated material. This could be a mosquito coil or an electronic or gas-powered insect killer. The power source is different, but they all disperse an insecticidal vapour. Depending on the model, you will need to replace the cartridge every few hours/days or top it up by adding some liquid insecticide. Burning mosquito coils shouldn't be used in a tent but the electric dispersers claim to be safe for humans and can be used indoors or in a tent.

Bears and other larger animals

If you're camping in bear country, or anywhere larger scavenging wildlife could be a problem, these are the USDA (United States Department of Agriculture) Forest Services recommendations. Some of these recommendations are law in some states but this varies around the world and the recommendations are good wherever you are:

◄ Keeping your tent well away from your cooking, food preparation and food storage areas is important in places where large scavenging animals may be present

and food containers look like and will break open a car to get at one if they can see it, even if they can't smell it.

● Keep a clean tent. Never bring any food, drink, scented toiletries, chewing gum, sunscreen, candles or insect repellent into the tent. Change out of your day clothes before entering the tent and store the clothes with your food.

● Use bear-proof rubbish containers, double-bag rubbish to help keep the smell contained and store it somewhere safe. This could be in the back of your car, in a bear-proof locker or, if this isn't possible, well away from your tent.

● Store all food, drinks, toiletries and other smelly items in bear-proof containers out of sight and away from your tent. Some bears have learned what coolers

● Choose a campsite away from water, animal trails and food sources such as fruit trees or berry bushes.

● Aim to cook at least 50m (164ft) away from your tent. Store food, waste and other attractive items at least 50m (164ft) away as well but not in the same place as where you cook.

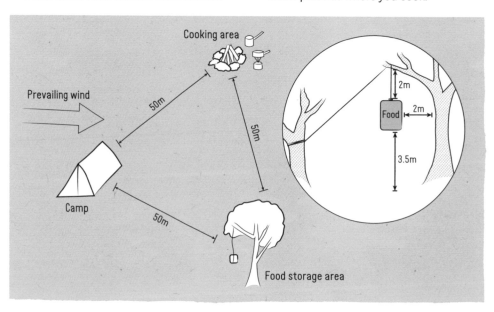

Nomadic working

Many jobs are now location-independent, requiring only a laptop, phone and a fast and reliable internet connection. You can work from anywhere, so why not work from your tent somewhere amazing? Unless you want to spend a lot of time (and money) sitting in cafes working, you'll need a campsite with electric hook-up, or your own reliable power source.

It's becoming increasingly common for campsites to have reasonable Wi-Fi across the entire site – you can check this before you arrive – although it doesn't guarantee a fast connection. You may have to pay to access the network and sometimes it only really works if you're close to the facilities block so if you're relying on site Wi-Fi for more than a couple of email checks, speak to the campsite and see if you can get a pitch with a good connection.

If the site has reasonable 4G (or, even better, 5G) mobile phone signal, you can connect a laptop to the internet through your phone, which normally offers faster download speeds and better security than a public Wi-Fi service. Be aware of the data limits of your contract, and if you expect to do this a lot, an unlimited data contract saves any worry or restriction. Depending on the specifics of your phone and laptop, you can normally connect simply by turning on the phone's personal hotspot in Settings and then connecting to the phone in the same way as you'd connect to any new Wi-Fi service. Multiple devices can be connected through the same phone.

To improve connection speed and reduce the drain on the battery and data

of your mobile phone, separate mobile hotspot devices or dongles are also available. These act very much like your home wireless router but connect to the 4G or 5G service using their own SIM and connection contract. You will have to buy the hotspot device and pay for the data like a mobile phone contract. They typically offer faster download speeds than a phone hotspot or a shared public Wi-Fi service; 5G hotspots can be faster than normal home broadband.

TOP TIP

TENT LIFE

1 Your sleeping system is essential for good sleep, and therefore an enjoyable camping trip. Consider every aspect, including what you sleep in and on.

2 Don't buy everything before your first camping trip. Make do with items you already have and then add to your collection of kit as you camp more and work out what works best for you. Camping chairs are great though – do get some.

3 Think about your requirements for water, power, heat and light before you go. Check what is available where you are staying and make sure you have the correct adaptors if you need any.

04

Fire and food

Gathering around a fire, creating a meal, sharing food and stories; evenings are one of the best times for camping. Even on solo adventures there are few better feelings than settling in for food and sleep, watching the sun set from the comfort of a tent after a long day out in the hills.

In this chapter, we'll cover all the basics of using fire to cook and stay warm while camping, along with some inspiration for choosing (or even finding) and preparing delicious food that works brilliantly cooked over a camping stove. We've been cooking outdoors for years, and we're gradually expanding our repertoire of dishes across the full spectrum, from lightweight yet satisfying quick-cook meals for when efficiency is a priority, through one-pot wonders for weekenders and family trips, to larger gatherings at which cooking outdoors is the main event.

Responsible campfires

Writing this after another hot, dry summer, during which wildfires blazed in many areas around the world and evidence emerged that several were started by campfires, stoves or barbeques, it's clear that fire has the potential to leave the worst scars. Far more than a trace.

Campsites either allow fires or they don't. Those that do require you to use a fire pit or bowl, or there will be a fire ring at each pitch for you to use. Most campsites prohibit the collection of firewood from the local area, so unless it's on sale at the site, you'll need to bring your own. Controlled campsite fires shouldn't therefore leave any further trace.

In wild places, and on any public land, with very, very few exceptions, there is no need to light a fire or to use any means of having a fire that leaves a trace, such as disposable fire pits/barbecues. At best, the black marks left in parks, on hills and by rivers look horrible. At worst, the fires can result in the destruction of large swathes of land and everything living there. The current plague of disposable barbecues is responsible for horrendous burns in young children and animals who stumble innocently upon them, black scars across the landscape, devastating wildfires, and toxic, unsightly litter. You can help by pushing for a total ban on disposable barbecues, including calling out shops that sell them, lobbying government and, of course, never using them. By contrast, modern camping stoves designed for backpacking use are light, packable, efficient and effective. Used properly, they're very safe and leave absolutely no trace.

▶ A steel fire bowl feels like an open campfire but protects the ground from damage

Fire safety

Cooking with fire is fun but can be hazardous – even more so if you're cooking near to tents. Lightweight nylon or polyester materials burn and melt easily and fiercely. If you're inside the tent when it happens, it's hard to escape. Even tents treated with a fire-retardant coating will burn – the treatment just slows the burn down, allowing more time to escape. And it's not just your tent: sleeping bags, mats and a lot of outdoor clothing is also extremely flammable and probably not treated with fire retardants. Even if you're cooking well away from your tent, stray sparks will quickly burn holes in your favourite down jacket. Natural materials such as cotton are more fireproof but will still burn if exposed to a flame.

▼ Open fires should be well contained and constantly supervised

Treating burns

SHOULD SOMEONE HAVE an accident, cool the burn under cool running water, or at the very least a container of cool or lukewarm water, as soon as you can. Keep it there for at least 20 minutes. The quicker you start cooling and the longer you do it for, the less severe the burn is likely to be.

Deep burns, chemical or electrical burns, burns that are larger than the size of your hand, burns that cause white or charred skin, burns to babies and children, and burns to the face or extremities of an adult that cause blistering all require urgent medical attention and may be considered an emergency. Seek help while continuing to cool the area. Medical treatment is also required if someone has inhaled smoke or fumes. For the full list, check online.

When the burn is cool, cover it with clingfilm or a clean plastic bag. This helps prevent infection by keeping the wound clean but won't stick to the burn. Stopping air getting to the burn also reduces the pain.

If clothing is stuck to the burn, do not try to remove it; you are likely to cause more damage.

In cold weather and particularly in a wilderness situation where medical extraction could take a significant amount of time, be aware that hypothermia caused by cooling the burn could become a problem. Try to cool just the burn rather than a larger area, while keeping the person warm.

Open fires are the least controllable – they can spread quickly, especially on dry ground, and are most likely to emit sparks. Stoves are generally safer as they tend to have a controlled and clean flame, but they can still be knocked over. The priming process required when lighting a liquid fuel stove can create a much larger and sometimes unexpected flame – don't lose your eyebrows by standing too close (as Sim once did).

If you're using a wood burner with a flue, a spark arrestor – a mesh cage that fits on to the top of the flue – will help to prevent sparks escaping and blowing on to your or someone else's tent.

When using gas or liquid fuel stoves, check the fuel is properly connected and sealed before lighting the stove as leaking fuel can ignite outside the container.

Always store spare gas and fuel away from the tent, fire and cooking area.

Depending on your set-up and available space/weight-carrying ability, consider keeping the following to hand when you are cooking with fire:

- A bucket of water.
- A fire blanket, placed within easy reach of the stove.
- A powder fire extinguisher – also handy to keep in the car.
- A tough, heat-resistant glove to return any escaped coals or sticks to the fire, or carry a hot pan safely.

Hygiene

Just because you're camping doesn't mean the pathogenic microbes are on holiday too. In an outdoor setting where mud, dust and insects are more prevalent, food can be harder to keep cool, and – if you do happen to fall ill – trips to the bathroom aren't exactly convenient, so practising good hygiene is perhaps even more important than it is at home.

Our hands are the biggest cause of cross-contamination so it's important to be able to wash them, before and during food preparation as well as before eating. If handwashing isn't available nearby, you can set up a hand cleaning station close to the camp – the Andy Handy spigot is an ingenious way to do this. A gravity-fed tap that releases a handful of water at a time when attached to a hanging water bag or bucket, it can be set alongside a small bar of soap in a mesh bag so it's easy for everyone to wash their hands whenever they need to.

Warm water makes washing-up not only more pleasant, especially in cold weather, but also much more effective. If there isn't a good supply nearby, it's

well worth heating a large pan of water specifically for the purpose. Even better, combine heating water for a round of hot drinks with heating water for washing-up. If you use a wood burning stove such as the Anevay Frontier or Petromax Loki, a hot water tank that wraps around the flue is a great addition, providing a ready supply of hot water on tap with no extra fuel usage.

▶ Andy Handy spigot

Cooking outdoors

Our human ancestors began cooking food somewhere between 400,000 and 1.8 million years ago. This practice began the gradual transition from a raw-food diet, from which energy would have been relatively difficult to extract, to a more energy-available cooked food diet. Today, many foods are highly processed, or at least pre-cooked, meaning the time and effort we need to put into food preparation is vanishingly small.

Cooking outdoors takes us back to our origins, reconnecting us with simpler times. Unlike our modern kitchens, where our hobs, ovens and microwaves are simply tools to get the job done, the joy of outdoor cooking lies in the methods used as much as in the food itself.

Fire

There's something about sitting around and cooking with fire – something that unites a primal desire for warmth, light and protection with a more personal nostalgia, companionship and sense of adventure. It doesn't matter if it's an open fire crackling in a pit or bowl, a storm kettle boiling away on the beach or a lightweight backpacking stove, it's the fire – its smell, sound, movement and immediacy – and the act of taming and tending it that never fails to ignite a thrill of excitement.

Campfires

Responsible campfires are best built in existing fire rings at campsites or below the high-water line of a tidal beach. A fire below the high tide line will still need supervision and proper cooling before you leave the site: kids and dogs run around on a beach and a partially covered but still hot fireplace can cause serious burns. There are some bushcraft techniques that you can use to build a fire and still leave a very minimal trace but honestly, we don't think an open fire in the wild is acceptable any more. If you're backpacking, the lightest stoves are so light that you can't use weight saving as an excuse for not taking one.

Fire pits or fire bowls

A great way of having a fire without damaging the ground is to use a fire pit or fire bowl. These contain the fire, lift it off the ground and sometimes aid the airflow, but the fire is still basically the same as a ground fire. Most fire pits and bowls are made from stainless steel because they must be tough and heat-resistant. This means they are heavy but will last for many years. Some designs, such as the Snow Peak Pack & Carry Fireplace, fold flat for easy transport; others are simpler solid bowls, which tend to be cheaper and work just as well – they just take up more room when not in use.

Camping stoves

A good camping stove allows you to cook food and heat water safely and effectively wherever your adventure takes you. There's a stove to suit every style of camping, from tiny lightweight and powerful burners to keep you fuelled on fast-and-light adventures, to dependable multi-fuel expedition units that will run on almost any liquid fuel and keep you going for months of use. Or, if space and weight aren't so much of an issue, there are single- and double-burner stoves, barbecues and pizza ovens that are perfect for a group meal outside. We've used so many different styles and brands of stove over the years. Some are still in regular use, some are kept for specific adventures, and some have pride of place on our shelf, brought out for special occasions only.

▶ MSR Dragonfly multi-fuel stove

▲ Solo stove

Solid fuel stoves

These stoves use solid fuel such as wood or charcoal to create heat for cooking or boiling water. Some types, such as the box stove and rocket stove, contain the fire within them and can be used to cook upon, whereas others, like the Dutch oven and reflector oven, must be placed in close proximity to the fire for cooking.

Box stoves

These are lightweight, folding stoves designed to burn wood or house and provide wind protection and pan support for an alcohol burner. They work in a similar way to a fire pit but are usually smaller and either fold or slide apart so that they can be packed flat. This means they are possible to

carry backpacking. Stainless-steel versions are heavier but more durable and cheaper than the lightweight titanium versions. A plus for a titanium box stove is that it cools down more quickly than steel so if you boil some water for lunch, you can pack the stove away and continue your walk. Box stoves burn well, providing wind protection and a chimney effect that draws air through the fire, making it burn hot. If you use an ash pan and place the stove on bare earth or a rock, then you can have a responsible fire in the wild.

Solo stoves

These make a simple but very effective mini fire pit that allows you to have a

▼ Rocket stove

responsible fire and cook easily. The twin-wall design creates hot fire due to the small combustion chamber and excellent airflow. It heats up quickly and easily burns small twigs, pine cones etc. A pot sits on stove supports above the fire and it will boil water in less than ten minutes. Solo makes a larger stove for base camp, garden or group use as well as a lighter titanium version. Other brands make similar small wood burners that are light enough to take backpacking.

Rocket stoves

These powerful and efficient stoves are designed to burn wood and produce a hot flame for cooking. The squat, compact design means they are easy to carry in a vehicle and work well whether at base camp or in your garden. At about 30 x 30 x 30cm (12 x 12 x 12in) and 2–7kg (4lb 7oz–15lb 7oz) depending on the design and materials, they are too big to be carried on your back or by bike. The L-shaped burning chamber means you add fuel to the base of the fire and also provides a strong draw of air that keeps the fire hot. Most designs then have a cast-iron cooking surface that heats up quickly and can support a large pot.

Wood burners

Wood burning stoves provide spacious stovetop cooking that's ideal for outdoor use in good weather. They can also be installed in tents to provide heat and to cook on. Used inside, they require a flue or chimney, which normally passes through a silicone flushing in the tent fabric. Wood burners are best in cotton-style tents just in case you get any chimney sparks, which

▲ Log burner

means they are normally only used in bell tents, tipis and yurts.

Basic wood burners like the Frontier Stove function well and pack up into a small (50 x 30 x 30cm/20 x 12 x 12in) bag, but the lighter-weight metal doesn't stay hot for very long once the fire has died down. They work best with compressed logs and manufactured fire logs as wet or damp wood doesn't burn brilliantly and is smoky. Heavier and more expensive camping wood burners will stay hot for longer and tend to have a better seal on the entrance to stop smoke entering the tent.

Most wood burners have a flat top for cooking on. Water heaters are available that wrap around the bottom section of the chimney and take up very little stove-top space. It's great having a constant supply of hot water while camping but do remember to keep it topped up to prevent it boiling dry.

BioLite CampStove

This combines a traditional wood-fuelled stove with a clever heat exchanger that produces electricity. The power is used to drive a small fan, which helps the fire burn hot, allowing you to use most twigs and sticks even if they are a bit damp. Excess energy can be used to recharge a phone or other small device via a USB port. You

▼ Kelly kettle

▲ Biolite stove

▲ Dutch oven on Rocket stove

can cook with a pan on top of the stove or add the BioLite kettle for efficient water boiling. For effective cooking on this stove, it's important to have a good supply of fuel ready: the hot fire and small burning chamber mean that you have to feed the fire regularly to keep a good heat under a pan.

Storm kettles or Kelly Kettles

Simple yet genius, storm kettles comprise a double-walled metal cylindrical kettle with a small fire built in the base. The central hole that right through the container acts as a chimney, drawing air up from the base for a clean, hot burn and transferring heat effectively and efficiently from the inside outwards to the water in the kettle. As well as boiling water for hot drinks in just a few minutes, the fire can be used for cooking by placing a pan on top of the base once the kettle has been removed. The fire is kept fed by dropping small twigs down the chimney – kids love to help with this. Storm kettles are bulky but tough and versatile – great for longer-term wilderness camping and trips to the beach, especially on chilly winter days when they can boil up a brew rapidly.

Dutch ovens

Dutch ovens (also known as camp ovens) are brilliant for cooking on wood and charcoal fires. They can be suspended over the fire or placed directly on to hot embers or charcoal briquettes. Adding embers or briquettes to the lid creates an oven environment that's suitable for baking – a rare delight when camping. Have a look at the recipes section for some ideas of what to cook.

Reflector ovens

A handy addition to a firepit set-up, or placed next to an open fire, a reflector oven is a metal box that's wider and open at one end and narrower and closed off at the other. With the open side next to the fire, food placed on a shelf in the oven cooks through heat reflected from the sides, as well as directly from the flames. They're best suited to food that requires relatively short cooking times, such as cookies, individual pizzas and flatbreads. When not in use, reflector ovens flat pack for storage.

◀ Reflector oven

Accessories

COOKING OVER SOLID fuel is brilliantly simple; however, there are a few accessories that can make your life easier, safer and more enjoyable.

Tripods
Cooking over solid fuel often requires balancing a pot or pan on a rock or on top of the stove itself. A tripod allows you to hang the pan over the fire, meaning less risk of toppling and the pan is always in the optimum position. Dutch ovens and other cast iron pots can be hung from a tripod over an open fire. You can buy collapsible cast-iron tripods or make one out of wood at each camp.

Skewers and spits
Made from either fresh wood or steel, these allow you to cook everything from marshmallows to meat, fish and vegetables.

Heatproof gloves
Widely available, made from tough, heat- and fire-resistant leather or synthetic material, a pair of gloves for use while tending stoves and handling hot pans is essential.

Tongs
Useful for moving burning coals or embers as well as turning food while it's cooking and removing it ready for serving, a good pair of long-handled tongs saves a lot of time and effort – and dropped food.

Pot lifter
Usually made from cast iron, pot lifters allow you to lift the lids of cast iron pans safely. If you're cooking with a Dutch oven, a pot lifter is essential.

▶ (*Opposite*) Tripod and fire pit

Gas and liquid fuel stoves

Lightweight gas stoves

Lightweight and portable gas canister stoves are the most common, easiest to use and broadest category of camping stove. Available in a wide range of budget and performance options, they are suitable for everything from car camping to expedition or superlight race use. The only real limitation is that they don't really work below -20°C (-4°F), but then how often does anyone camp at that temperature?!

There are three main types of lightweight gas stove, and then a wide range of options within each type. Here, we will outline the key benefits and problems with each and make suggestions for the best use.

With all gas canister stoves it's important to make sure the canister is properly connected to the stove before you light it. If there is a small gas leak you can end up setting fire to the canister, which tends to be bad news. Screw the canister on tightly and listen for the high-pressure sound of gas escaping before you attempt to light it.

Top-mounted and system stoves can be unstable balanced on top of the gas canister and the consequence of one tipping over is not good. To make these stoves more stable you can use a stabiliser, which clips on to the bottom of the gas canister and provides a wider base. Most stoves come with one

▼ Cooking a simple supper on a lightweight top-mounted gas stove

of these and they are universal, so once you have one you can use it with all of your stoves. If you don't have one you can buy them separately. They only weigh about 25g (0.88oz).

Most stoves claim to only work with gas canisters manufactured by the same company; this isn't true, the valve is universal, but it may affect any warranty or other guarantee should you be using another brand and anything goes wrong. We have found that some manufacturers appear to use slightly more precise

▶ Alpkit remote canister gas stove and lightweight titanium pans

▼ Primus double burner

TOP TIP

HANGING KITS

In some circumstances, like when climbing or sailing, it's safer to hang your stove from something rather than trying to find a flat surface to balance it on. Hanging kits allow you to suspend a stove safely (ish, but safer than the alternatives) from a single point and then cook on them. Top-mounted gas stoves or system stoves can be adapted to do this and some manufacturers such as Jetboil, MSR and Primus produce hanging kits designed specifically for their stoves.

tolerances when making the stove and the canisters than others, which can mean that occasionally you will get a stove and canister that are hard to fit together perfectly. We have only ever experienced this with a stove and gas canister made by different manufacturers. It's always worth doing a test fit and light in the garden before you take a gas stove away on a trip, just in case.

Top-mounted canister stoves

These little gas stoves are essentially a burner and pot support that fits directly on top of the gas canister.

Pros: They are lightweight, normally less than 100g (3.5oz) with the lightest about 25g (0.88oz). They have a small pack size, with the pot supports folding in on themselves. They can also be powerful, and some can boil 1 litre (1.8 pints) of water in around three minutes (although this depends on conditions). Even the lightest stoves, commonly have a piezo ignition system. These are often the cheapest stoves although expensive materials like titanium and high-performance low-weight versions can be pricey.

Cons: They are susceptible to the wind and will work much more efficiently in low- or no-wind conditions. Stability can be an issue as they tend to have small and lightweight pot supports so they are best used with small pots. The small burner isn't so good with larger pans or frying pans as it tends to spot-heat rather than spreading the heat across the base of the pan.

Remote canister stoves

These gas stoves have a burner unit and pot support that stands on the floor with a pipe and valve that allows the gas to be positioned away from the stove.

Pros: This can allow a more stable design that can cope with larger pots. Slightly larger units have powerful burners that heat quickly and work with larger pots. It's more windproof and you can use a close-fitting wind shield around the burner without

◀ MSR WindPro remote canister stove by Scott Rinckenberger

▲ Multiple stoves can be used when cooking for a larger group

risking overheating the gas. Some remote canister stoves can run on liquid gas from an inverted gas canister, which improves performance in low temperatures.

Cons: Heavier and bulkier than a top-mounted stove but lightweight versions are still less than 200g (7oz) and fit inside a 1 litre (1.8 pint) pot. Tend to cost more than top-mounted stoves.

System stoves

These stoves are normally top mounted on a gas canister but the stove, windbreak and pan are all one system. Together, they are designed to offer an efficient and fast boil time. They often lock together, making them more stable than an equivalent top-mounted stove, although the whole system could fall over.

Pros: Efficient use of gas and fast boil times achieved with a combination of close-fitting pan and burner, good integrated wind protection and heat exchanger pan units.

Cons: Often heavier than a light top-mounted stove and lightweight pan but reduced gas use may mean you don't need to carry as much gas. More expensive than other styles of gas stoves even if you include buying a separate pan. These work best with the integrated pan and are best used for boiling water rather than more gourmet cooking.

Group and family stoves

When you're catering for a group it's much easier to use larger pans and cook on a sturdier set-up. A good group stove will be solid and dependable, easily able

Piezo ignition

SOME GAS STOVES feature an integrated piezo-electric igniter. This is a small device that produces a spark, so you don't need a lighter or matches. Inside the igniter there is a small spring-loaded hammer and a lead zirconate titanate crystal. When the crystal is hit by the hammer, it releases an electrical charge in response to the mechanical deformation. The charge is the spark that ignites the gas.

In our experience, piezo igniters are brilliant while they last, but they may not last as long as the stove. For this reason, it's always worth carrying another source of ignition just in case the lighter does fail. Replacement piezo igniters are available from the stove manufacturers and can be used to repair your stove once you get home.

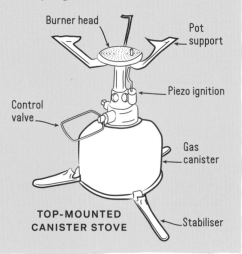

TOP-MOUNTED CANISTER STOVE

to accommodate a couple of large pans without feeling like it's going to collapse. If you go into any camping shop, you'll find a selection of double-burner stoves perfect for group or family use. Most of these open with the lid and sides creating a windbreak when in use and protecting the burners when in transport. Some include a grill underneath, which adds some versatility, though they are never as good as the one at home. That said, they will produce a serviceable cheese on toast.

Some of these larger stoves come as a unit with extendable legs, while others are simply the stove, ready for use on a table, tailgate or the floor. If the stove doesn't have legs, there are lots of camping kitchen units available designed to support a double-burner stove; some will also have a couple of useful shelves underneath for pans and utensils.

The burners will be rated in watts (power) with a higher rating normally meaning a quicker boil time and faster gas consumption. Most group stoves will produce between 1,500W and 4,500W or 1.5kW and 4.5kW. Some stoves will have ways of making the burner more efficient with wind protection or heat exchangers and will therefore have a lower power output, longer gas life and similar boil times. In our experience, there isn't normally a lot of difference in boil times or gas usage between these stoves so choose the one with the features and design that works for you.

Most stoves of this kind run from a large, refillable butane or propane canister. The blue Campingaz 907 or 904 are the most common types in the UK and Europe, but different canisters are available worldwide. Most stoves will run on any of these gases, but you will have to have the correct regulator. You can usually buy a regulator wherever you can get gas and it's easy to change with a screwdriver.

Some higher-quality double-burner camping stoves use small screw on-gas canisters like the lightweight gas stoves. This is great for a weekend, but space and weight are still important as the gas is much smaller and lighter than the big refillable canisters. It is more expensive to use the small canisters and although they can be recycled, you are still producing waste. Most of these stoves can run on refillable gas canisters if you get an adapter to allow them to be connected, so if you regularly use the stove when weight and space aren't an issue, get an adapter and a refillable canister.

Gas-fuelled pizza ovens and barbeques

In addition to double-burner group stoves, there are several more specialist cooking options that are too heavy for anything but car camping or a base camp. These include barbecues, grills and pizza ovens that are great for garden use as well as for taking on camping trips. They extend the repertoire of camp cooking and can create a special evening meal.

Most of this type of cooker run off the large, refillable gas canisters like the double-burners, while some models can also run off solid fuel. If you're using multiple larger stoves it's a good idea to get a matching regulator and make sure they will work from the same source to save having to cart around multiple canisters.

▼ Portable gas pizza oven

Liquid fuels and multi-fuel stoves

Liquid fuels are petroleum-based and include Coleman fuel (also known as white gas), kerosene, diesel, petrol and aviation fuels. Stoves that will burn these fuels are useful for travelling to areas where camping gas isn't readily available. We are not including alcohol-based fuels in this section as the stoves work in a different way. These fuels are available worldwide and are cheaper than gas. Multi-fuel stoves can run on most different liquid fuels. Some, like the Primus Omnifuel and the Optimus Polaris Optifuel, also have a valve to allow them to use gas canisters.

Another option popular with overland vehicle expeditions and for use at an expedition base camp is the Coleman two-burner stove. This compact and powerful stove runs on unleaded petrol or Coleman fuel, which means that fuel is cheap (compared to gas canisters) and easily available worldwide. The stoves are very tough and dependable but slightly smellier and more effort than a gas canister.

The process of pressurising, heating and burning liquid fuels is a bit more complicated than a gas burner so these stoves tend to be a bit heavier and bulkier. The lightest are close to 300g (10.6oz) so they aren't very heavy, except in comparison to some gas stoves that are less than 50g (1.8oz). The fuel bottle will always be remote (attached to the stove by a fuel line rather than attaching directly to the burner), so they can be used with a close-fitting wind shield and often accommodate larger pans. Liquid fuel stoves are not affected by low temperatures or high altitudes because you can maintain the fuel pressure. For all these reasons, liquid fuel stoves are most common for longer expeditions or travel in more remote areas.

Due to their extra size and bulk, along with a more complicated lighting process, dirtier fuel and flame, and added requirement for maintenance, most people wouldn't take a liquid fuel stove camping for a short trip in good conditions where gas is easily available. They do work perfectly well in these conditions, though, so if you only buy one stove and plan to use it in cold, high or inaccessible areas too, this is the style to get.

Safety notes

CAUTION: Always use a specifically designed fuel bottle rather than, for example, a metal drinking bottle. Fuel bottles are designed to withstand the internal pressure created when pressurising the fuel for use. They have a maximum fill line, which you shouldn't exceed when filling, maintaining enough air in the tank to create the pressure needed for efficient use. They are also red and clearly labelled so that you don't mix it up and take a drink...

◄ MSR Dragonfly multi-fuel stove in the Cascades by Scott Rinckenberger

Coleman fuel, kerosene, unleaded petrol and aviation fuels tend to be purer and burn cleaner than diesel. Most liquid fuel stoves will run on any of these fuels, but most will use a slightly larger burner jet for the dirtier fuels. If you are going to be using diesel or another less pure liquid fuel, you will need to swap the small jet that is normally pre-installed for the larger jet. This reduces the likelihood of blockages caused by the impurities in the fuel. There will be instructions on how to do this for your individual stove and most stoves come with the spare jet and tools you need.

Liquid fuel stoves work by pressurising the fuel and heating it, turning it into a gas; the burning gas is what you cook on. Stoves need to be primed before you can cook, a process that requires heating up the boiler tube by lighting a small, controlled fire to get it hot enough to vaporise the fuel.

To light and use a liquid fuel stove, follow these basic instructions. Different stoves will work and set up differently, so check the instructions for your specific model, but the main process is the same. Be aware that the initial priming will normally involve a brief flare of flame, which can be 30cm (12in) high. Always cook and use a stove away from flammable items and ideally outside.

1   Make sure there is enough fuel in the tank and connect the stove, pump and fuel tank together. Make sure the pump and fuel tube are correctly attached. Set up the heat shield and windbreak ready for use.

2   Check all valves are set to 'off'. Pump the tank until you reach sufficient pressure,

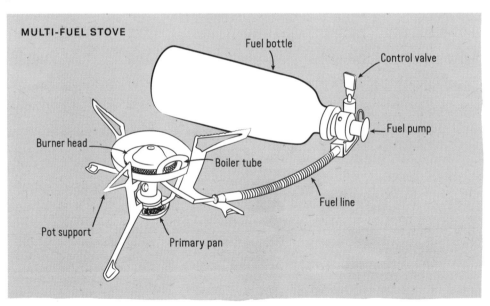

MULTI-FUEL STOVE

Fuel bottle

Control valve

Fuel pump

Burner head

Boiler tube

Fuel line

Pot support

Primary pan

Strip and clean the stove regularly ... it's worth doing a test at home before you have to work out how to take it apart halfway up a mountain.

normally about 20 strokes but this varies with the size and fill of the bottle.

3   If you are using Coleman fuel, kerosene or petrol, open the valve for a couple of seconds to allow a small amount of liquid fuel into the priming pan. If you are using diesel, pour a small amount of priming fuel into the priming pan. Close the valve again.

4   Light the fuel and allow it to burn (it normally flares up). Just before the flame dies, open the valve. This will allow fuel to keep the flame alight and should quickly result in a strong blue roaring flame. It is normal to get a flare when you first open the valve as the last of the liquid fuel burns off and before the gas starts to feed the flame.

5   Cook your food or heat your water. You will probably need to add about ten pumps of pressure every ten minutes or so. If the flame starts to stutter or flare yellow, this is a sign of low pressure.

6   When you've finished, simply turn off the fuel at the pump. This allows any remaining fuel in the fuel line to burn off. When the stove goes out, close the stove valve as well and allow the stove to cool.

Troubleshooting

The different types of fuels and multiple parts of a liquid fuel stove mean there are a few bits that need attention and can go wrong. Helpfully, because these stoves are designed for expedition use, most can be stripped and fixed quite easily and will come with a few spares, a jet pricker and the tools you need. Parts are available and most manufacturers sell a service kit that includes the common washers, O-rings, pump cups and oil that you need to keep a stove going. For long trips, it's a

TROUBLESHOOTING LIQUID FUEL STOVES

Problem	Fix
Leaking fuel between the pump and bottle or pump and fuel line	Clean the joint and replace the washer or O-ring.
Erratic and yellow flames	Often due to improper preheating. Repeat the priming sequence.
No pressure after pumping	Replace the fuel pump cup, clean, and try again.
Plunger hard to pump	Clean and lubricate the pump cup.
Low or stuttering flames	This may be low fuel pressure. Add ten pumps.
Slow boiling times, reduced performance	Check and clean the fuel jet and fuel line.
Low or stuttering flames at altitude	This can be caused by insufficient airflow; try opening the windshield slightly.

good idea to take a whole spare pump as well, as these are often more delicate and likely to go wrong than the stove itself. If you predominantly use Coleman fuel you probably won't have to strip and clean the stove very often or if it gets used regularly, ever. If you use dirtier fuel like diesel you will have to strip and clean the stove regularly. Individual stoves will have instructions on how to do this. They are all similar but it's worth doing a test at home before you have to work out how to take it apart halfway up a mountain.

Alcohol-based fuel and stoves

First, a word of caution: unlike traditional gas camping stoves, the flame of an alcohol stove is silent and almost invisible. This makes accidental burns more likely as there's little warning that the stove is lit. Never leave a burning alcohol stove unattended.

Alcohol stoves are very simple burners with a way of supporting a pot over them. You pour alcohol into the burner and light it, cooking on the heat it produces. Because they're simple they can be very light – often less than 50g (1.8oz). They are also easy to use and durable, with no moving parts or tubes to block or break. The fuel is easily available, but it releases less energy than gas or liquid petroleum fuels when burned so will be slower to bring water to the boil.

Pros: Alcohol stoves are lightweight, quiet, simple, durable, cheap and the fuel is cheap and easily available.

Cons: They are slower at boiling water, susceptible to light winds and are harder to use at low temperatures. On longer trips, they can become heavier because the fuel is less efficient, so you must carry more volume.

There are many designs of stove to buy or even make yourself:

- The Trangia is the classic dependable alcohol stove with a lightweight burner that's supported in a cleverly designed windshield and pot support. The burner, windshield, pans and lid all pack into themselves. The 27 series is designed for one to two people, while the 25 series is slightly bigger and designed for two to four people. There's also a Mini Trangia, designed for one person. All use the same brass burner, which weighs 111g (3.9oz) on its own. The 27 and 25 series models come as a set with two saucepans, a lid/frying pan and a windshield, while the Mini has a lightweight pot support and single pan with a lid/frying pan. Some sets come with a kettle included, or you can buy the kettle separately.

- For a super-light alcohol burner, Vargo makes three titanium models weighing between 24g (0.85oz) and 38g (1.34oz). The titanium makes them light and strong but doesn't conduct heat as well as the brass Trangia burner, so they take a little while longer to get going. Priming them with a little extra fuel and a shallow priming dish helps.

- The Evernew titanium burner looks more like a Trangia burner but weighs 36g (1.27g). It burns well but users report it being more fuel-hungry than other alcohol burners.

- You can even make your own alcohol burner out of one or two tin cans. If you search for 'hobo stoves' on the internet you will find a whole host of different designs. We've tested a design called the sideburner, which works well and weighs about 10g (0.35oz).

Alcohol is often bought and can be transported in lightweight plastic bottles. It's safe to use these bottles on a camping trip, although labelling fuel bottles is always a good idea to prevent any mistakes.

◀ Trangia stove

Alcohol doesn't ignite until it gets hot enough. In warmer weather, a lighter or match is able to warm the alcohol enough for it to light, but in cold weather you may need to warm it first. If it's cold, carrying the stove and fuel in an inside pocket for a while before use makes a big difference. A priming pan can then be used to warm the stove and alcohol before lighting the stove. To do this, sit the stove in a shallow fireproof dish, pour in a small amount of fuel and light it. It should be easier to light the smaller volume of fuel in the priming pan than the burner. This fuel will warm the stove and the fuel to a point that allows you to light it more easily. Once lit, give the stove a few seconds to fully heat up before you place the pan on top, otherwise the cooling effect of the cold pan may reduce the temperature enough to put the stove out. If it's cold, it's also worth placing your stove on a more insulating surface such as wood to help with efficient lighting and burning.

Bear in mind that many areas, in particular National Parks and other wild areas over the drier months, have fire bans in place to protect the land and its inhabitants. Unlike gas stoves, alcohol stoves do not have a valve that can be used to shut off the flame. As a result, they are specifically banned in some areas so check and consider carefully before use.

▼ Scout helping to cook a meal on a trusty Trangia

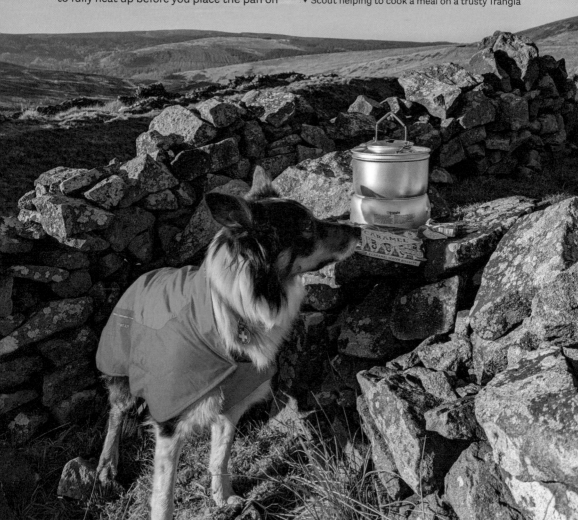

Solid fuel hexamine stoves

Originally designed as emergency stoves for military or survival use, these small and compact stoves burn solid fuel hexamine tablets (hexamethyl-enetetramine or methenamine). These burn hot and cleanly with almost no residue or ash left over. The fumes can be toxic, so it's important to use these stoves outdoors and never in a tent. If kept in its waterproof wrapping, the fuel will last a long time, making these a good emergency stove to leave packed in a car, boat or an emergency pack.

The classic Esbit pocket stove has been in production since 1936 and although the newer versions are neater, the design is essentially the same. Weighing about 90g (3.2oz) and constructed from strong, galvanised steel, they are extremely durable and well made. The fuel tablets pack up inside when you fold them closed. There are lots of cheaper copies that work effectively and cost less than £10; all burn the same fuel tablets.

In use, hexi stoves are simple to set up and easy to light. The fuel tablets burn hot, so if you create some wind shelter you can boil water in less than five minutes, similar to a gas or liquid fuel stove and a bit quicker than alcohol. You can't really vary the temperature, so these are best for heating water, in which you can heat pouches of ready-to-eat food or use with dehydrated meal pouches, rather than trying to cook more complicated meals. If the fuel is running out, you can add more while it's still alight.

Hexi fuel also works well as a firelighter if you have a wood burning stove and you're struggling to get it to light, although they are more expensive than normal firelighters.

▲ Esbit Pocket Stove

Getting the most from your camping stove

Whichever stove and fuel you use, if you can maximise the efficiency of the system, you can cook your food more quickly and use less fuel overall.

Use the correct stove

Even the best canister gas stoves won't perform well below about -22°C (-7.6°F), so if you're travelling to very cold places, you'll need to use a liquid fuel stove. If the temperatures are above 10°C (50°F), a butane-rich gas mix will be more efficient.

Lids

When you're boiling or simmering water or food, always use a lid (a piece of kitchen foil works well as a lightweight option) and as far as possible avoid opening the lid. You can hear when water starts to boil so you don't need to keep opening the lid to check.

Windproofing

According to stove manufacturers MSR, when using an open flame stove (like an MSR PocketRocket) with no windproofing, an 8km/h (5mph) wind will treble the time it takes to boil. So, it's very important to windproof your stove as much as possible. Many stoves have built-in wind protection, but they will still benefit from a sheltered spot. Try to create a sheltered cooking area using the terrain and equipment you have. You can position tents, vehicles, tarp windbreaks and rucksacks to create a sheltered cooking area, or use a flexible windbreak around liquid or remote canister stoves. Don't use a windbreak that also encloses the gas canister or fuel source as this can cause excess heating of the fuel. For top-mounted canister stoves, clip-on windbreaks that protect the stove and base of the pan without reaching the ground and enclosing the gas are the best option.

Pressure regulator

If you're using a canister gas stove, a good pressure regulator ensures the stove continues to burn well, even when the gas is running low. Using the maximum amount of gas possible and maintaining a good output is more efficient than using a stove that struggles to use the canister when the pressure drops.

Heat exchanger pans

Pans with a heat exchanger built into the base increase the amount of heat retained and can improve efficiency by up to about a third. Most stove systems (examples include Jetboil, MSR WindBurner and Primus Lite Plus) use these pans, but you can also buy them separately to be used on other styles of stove. They are slightly bulkier, harder to clean and more expensive than a normal pan.

The correct fuel mix and canister design

If you plan to use a gas canister stove in cold conditions (less than 5°C/41°F), winter-specific fuel mixes will help the stove run most efficiently. Gas canisters can also be designed to improve their efficiency at lower temperatures. The Primus Winter Gas canister has a lining that collapses as the canister empties: this increases the surface area from which the liquid gas can evaporate, helping to keep the internal pressure higher and improving the output.

Insulating canisters

As a stove is used, the process of the liquid gas in a canister evaporating cools the canister. A cold canister will have a lower internal pressure and requires more energy for the gas to evaporate. If you insulate the canister from the cold ground, you reduce the heat loss of the canister due to conduction and therefore keep the internal pressure higher. A small piece of closed cell foam camping mat works well for this.

Warming a gas canister

A cold canister has lower internal pressure and is therefore less efficient. In cold conditions, if you warm a gas canister before use by keeping it in an inside pocket or in your sleeping bag then the pressure will be higher initially. If you have two canisters in rotation, you can warm one while the other is in use, and when the stove's performance drops because the canister has cooled, you can switch canisters and continue cooking. While the stove is on, you can warm the canister by wrapping your hands around it. Some people place the canister in a pan and add warm water to keep the canister warmer – this can work well if the water stays warm, but if it doesn't you are just cooling the gas. If you are warming the canister, be very careful never to make it hot; it should always be comfortable to touch.

Inverted cylinders

Some gas canister stoves are designed to be able to invert the canister and convert the liquid gas into fuel in the stove system. This allows the gas stoves to be used in colder conditions, but the stove must be designed specifically to do this.

◀ MSR WindPro stove in the Cascades by Scott Rinckenberger

Fuel

There are several different fuels that camping stoves can run on and understanding the benefits of each can help to decide which stove is best for your expedition. Small gas canisters are light, fast and clean but gas isn't reliably available worldwide, and if you are away for a longer trip, the cost, weight and bulk of the gas can quickly add up. Larger, more economical, refillable gas canisters are great for vehicle camping but too heavy for anything else. Liquid fuel stoves are powerful, work anywhere and you can get cheap fuel worldwide, but they are initially expensive, heavier than gas canister stoves and require more maintenance. Alcohol stoves are tough, simple and dependable but a bit slow and they don't like very cold weather. Solid fuel stoves that use fuel tablets, wood pellets or scavenged wood can be very light, and you may not have to carry fuel, but they are harder to control, have a dirtier flame and are harder to use in bad weather.

We use gas canister stoves for fast-and-light weekend excursions when overall weight and cooking speed is important, and multi-fuel stoves for longer expedition-style missions or when we are travelling outside of western Europe and North America. We use a double-burner with a large refillable gas canister for family camping and base camp use, and our alcohol burning Trangia and wood burning Kelly Kettle come on beach and chilled-out backpacking adventures when we have time to cook and don't need to carry things too far.

Fuel availability worldwide

The type of fuel available at your destination may be the main reason you decide to take a certain type of stove. Here is a rough guide to the types of fuel available worldwide. Liquid fuel, such as kerosene or diesel, is the most widely available type so liquid fuel stoves are most popular when travelling outside of Europe and North America. The MSR XGK stove has been specifically designed to work well with less-pure or lower-quality liquid fuels often found in remote areas. Often, gas canisters and Coleman fuel are available in popular expedition areas such as Patagonia or the Himalayas but would be harder to find in the less popular areas of the same country – e.g. you may struggle to find gas canisters in other areas of Argentina or central India.

If you need single-use gas canisters for your stove, try to avoid buying refilled ones. It is possible to refill these gas canisters but it's very hard to completely refill them. One way to check is to weigh them, although that's likely to be hard to do. Refilled canisters are not as safe as new ones as the valve and screw thread will have had a lot more use than they were designed for and therefore are more likely to leak. Sometimes the canisters are refilled with pure propane, which can be dangerous, especially in warmer climates. Standard canisters are not strong enough for the internal pressure propane can produce so they could explode in normal warm temperatures.

It's very useful to know the local name for the type of fuel you need so do check before you leave. We've included some of the popular names for the same fuels in the table below.

How much fuel?

When you're car camping and space isn't an issue, it's easy to throw in an extra gas canister or bottle of fuel, just in case. Even if you do find yourself running out of fuel, you can probably just wander over to the on-site shop and buy some more so you probably don't need to worry too much about calculating exactly how much you'll need. However, when space and weight are

an issue, you really don't want to be carrying an extra gas canister, or even just a bigger canister than you will need. Or, if you're on a longer trip where resupply is unlikely to be an option, how do you work out how much fuel you will need to see you through?

To calculate your daily fuel consumption, you need to know how many people you are feeding and how many hot meals and hot drinks you will prepare for them each day. Use these numbers to work out roughly how many litres or pints of water you need to boil per day. If food or drink doesn't need to be boiled to be cooked, still count it as a boil as it's unlikely to have required much

FUEL AVAILABILITY WORLDWIDE

Type of fuel	Availability
Screw-on gas canisters	Europe, North America, Australia, South Africa, specialist camping shops worldwide
Large Campingaz 907 and 904 refills	Europe
Other large refillable gas canisters	Worldwide but specific to countries or regions so you may need to source a regulator at the same time to be sure it will work
Coleman fuel, naphtha, sheltie or white gas	Europe, North America, Australia, South Africa, specialist camping shops worldwide
Kerosene or paraffin	Everywhere although the quality can be lower in some areas so you may have to clean your stove more often
Diesel	Worldwide but like kerosene, the quality varies
Petrol	Worldwide but like kerosene, the quality varies. Petrol is not as good fuel for a stove as kerosene or diesel because fuel additives are more commonly used, which require you to clean the valves more often
Denatured alcohol, methylated spirits, rubbing alcohol, grain alcohol, HEET gasoline additive	Worldwide but it's helpful to know its local name as it's often used for something other than stove fuel

▶ A powerful single burner gas stove designed for group use and larger pans

less fuel and we think it's better to come home with a little fuel left than to run out. Most stove manufacturers give a water boiled per volume/weight of fuel figure in the stove spec sheets, so you can use this to work out how much fuel you need.

WATER BOILED PER VOLUME/ WEIGHT OF FUEL FOR DIFFERENT STOVE TYPES

Stove type	Average volume of water boiled per 100g/100ml (3.5fl oz) of fuel
Top-mounted gas stove	7 litres (12.3 pints)
Remote canister gas stove	8 litres (14 pints)
Gas system stove	8.5 litres (15 pints)
Liquid fuel stove – kerosene	5.5 litres (9.7 pints)
Liquid fuel stove – white gas	5 litres (8.8 pints)
Alcohol stove	2 litres (3.5 pints)

* The table above assumes normal rather than winter conditions and the efficient use of the stove. If you are using the stove in cold winter conditions, high altitudes or having to melt snow to create water, you can easily use three to four times the amount of gas suggested above. Temperature and altitude will affect liquid fuel stoves less but if you are melting snow, you may still need to double these figures.

Gas

Gas canisters

Gas canisters are available in a variety of sizes, connections and gas blends. Most gas stoves can use a range of sizes and blends of gas, but the connection is specific to the stove. The most common connection for lighter-weight stoves is a screw-on connection. They are self-sealing so you can take them off the stove without losing the gas. These are made by several brands and are normally available in three sizes measured by the weight of gas they contain (net weight). The standard-size canisters contain around 100g (3.5oz), 230g (8.1oz) or 450g (15.9oz) of gas but some manufacturers produce canisters that hold slightly more or less gas, as you can see in the table overleaf.

GAS CANISTER WEIGHTS

Net fuel weight on canister	Gross full canister weight*	Empty canister weight*
100g (3.5oz)	200g (7oz)	100g (3.5oz)
110g (3.9oz)	212g (7.5oz)	102g (3.5oz)
220g (7.8oz)	367g (12.9oz)	147g (5.2oz)
230g (8.1oz)	390g (13.8oz)	160g (5.6oz)
440g (15.5oz)	598g (21oz)	158g (5.6oz)
450g (15.9oz)	645g (22.8oz)	195g (6.9oz)

*All weights are averages after weighing several different brands' canisters.

The popular single-burner car camping stove and some heaters and other stoves use an aerosol-shaped self-sealing gas canister that uses a push-on rather than a screw-on valve. These canisters are normally 220g (7.8oz) net weight.

Campingaz also makes press-on, self-sealing gas canisters that look a lot like the normal screw-on style. They are available in 240g (8.5oz) or 450g (15.9oz) net weights. They only work with the Campingaz push-fit stoves and are not compatible with screw-on stoves.

Some older-style and cheaper gas stoves use a gas canister without a valve. When you first install it, the stove pierces the canister so it can't be removed until empty. Campingaz are the main supplier of these C206 canisters. A big advantage of this system is that the gas is cheap and much more widely available worldwide than any of the other styles of disposable canister.

All of the above styles of canister are single-use and can't be refilled. When gas canisters are almost empty, they produce a much less powerful flame, so they are annoying to cook with, especially if you're really hungry. If you aren't sure how much gas is left in a canister you can weigh it – the canister will always say the net weight of gas that it contained when new, so if you know the canister weight, you can work out how much gas is left. The table above can help with this. If you don't know the canister weight but know the gross weight (gas plus canister when new), subtract the net weight from the gross weight to find the canister weight.

We tend to take a new or almost new canister backpacking or on more space- or

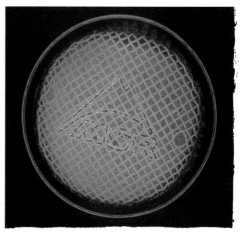

▲ The MSR Reactor viewed from above, a very efficient system stove

▶ Gas stove with canister support

weight-critical adventures. We take the emptier ones on slower camping trips when we have space for several canisters. When we are car camping, it usually doesn't matter if it takes 20 minutes to boil a pan of water. Our Primus Tupike double-burner and MSR Reactor Stove System are both good at running on nearly empty gas, whereas some stoves really struggle. When the canister is empty, use a Jetboil CrunchIt to empty and pierce the canister, which means it can be recycled with normal aluminium cans.

Large, refillable gas canisters work with most group camping double-burner-style stoves and some barbecues and pizza ovens. These canisters are more expensive to buy initially, but once you have a canister, you can swap the empty one for a full canister for about half the price of the initial purchase. Campingaz in particular has a good worldwide dealer network, so it is often possible to find replacement gas canisters outside of Europe and North America. It typically takes two refills before this is a cheaper way of cooking than single-use canisters, and you aren't producing any waste. These canisters will have a self-sealing valve so you can disconnect them for storage or travel. They will almost always require a regulator specific to the style of gas canister. The regulator controls the amount of gas travelling from the canister to the stove and is specific to the type of gas rather than the stove. If the stove doesn't come with a regulator or you need a different one to use a different style of gas canister, they are not expensive and can be changed with a screwdriver.

Gas mixtures

Gas stoves will burn butane, isobutane or propane or a mixture of these gases. Each gas has different characteristics making it better for specific conditions, and manufacturers mix the gases to try to make the canisters work well in a wider range of these. The gas inside the canister is under high pressure so the gas is stored as liquid: as you release the pressure by turning on the stove, the liquid evaporates and escapes to be burned at the stove. The conversion of the liquid to gas requires energy, which is why gas canisters feel cold during use.

The different gases have different boiling points as shown in the table below. If the ambient temperature where you are trying to cook is below the boiling point of the gas it won't evaporate, and your stove won't work. Conversely, the higher the ambient temperature above the gas boiling point, the higher the pressure in the canister. A canister under high pressure will release more gas as you cook, which is inefficient. Ultimately, if you are in a very hot environment with a full propane gas canister, you may come close to the maximum pressure the canister is designed to resist. Propane camping canisters shouldn't be stored in temperatures over 40°C (104°F). There isn't a danger of them exploding until much higher temperatures (more like 150°C/302°F) but once you get over 40°C (104°F), the pressure release valve may start to let some propane escape to reduce the internal pressure.

THE BOILING POINTS OF GASES

	Boiling point*
Butane	-2°C (28.4°F)
Isobutane	-11.7°C (10.94°F)
Propane	-42°C (-43.6°F)

* The boiling point is the temperature at which a liquid becomes gas under normal atmospheric pressure.

The manufacturers of the gas canisters use either a pure gas or a mixture to create a gas suitable for use in a specific temperature range:

- Summer mixes are normally butane and propane, designed to work best from 10°C (50°F) to around 40°C (104°F).
- All-season mixes are normally isobutane and propane, designed to work best from about -10°C (14°F) to 20°C (68°F).
- Winter mixes are normally isobutane and propane, designed to work best between around -20°C (-4°F) and 5°C (41°F).

You can't get lightweight propane-only gas canisters because they can't be made strong enough to safely withstand temperatures that may be encountered during the summer months. Therefore, lightweight canisters designed for cold weather use contain a mix of propane and isobutane, meaning they'll also be safe in higher temperatures. Larger, refillable propane gas canisters are available for use with group camping stoves and barbeques. These are much heavier and stronger so they can withstand higher pressures.

Gas regulators

Regulators control the pressure of the gas entering the burner. For stoves that use large gas canisters, a separate regulator must be used. These attach to the top of the canister and regulate the gas travelling down the hose to the burner. Stoves that run off small canisters, including most backpacking stoves, can have a regulator integrated into the stove unit but this isn't always the case. If the stove doesn't have a regulator, then the stove burns gas at the canister pressure, which changes depending on the temperature, altitude and how full or empty the canister is. Stoves with regulators are designed to run at lower pressures than stoves without regulators, which means that they run better and have less noticeable decline in power when it's cold, or when the gas canister is less than half full. A good-quality gas regulator will continue to deliver the full power output of the stove for most of the gas canister's life. The downside of a regulated stove is that quality regulators rely on precise engineering, which is more expensive to develop, so the stoves cost more. They are also slightly bulkier and heavier, but this is only noticeable in superlight stoves. The MSR PocketRocket Deluxe has a regulator and weighs just 83g (2.9oz), 10g (0.35oz) heavier than the PocketRocket 2, which doesn't have a

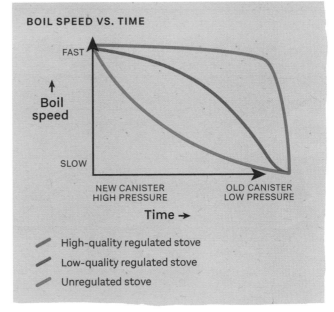

BOIL SPEED VS. TIME

High-quality regulated stove
Low-quality regulated stove
Unregulated stove

regulator or piezo ignition. The Deluxe does cost about 40 per cent extra, though.

This graph shows the performance over time of gas canister stoves with and without regulator control.

WHAT TO COOK ON AND HOW TO COOK IN EVERY CAMPING SITUATION

1 There is a stove or fire solution for every adventure, from super-light gas or alcohol stoves to fire pits and pizza ovens. As with all kit, if you can work out what you are likely to use most and get that, you can adapt it for most situations.

2 Plan and keep it simple; when you know what you will be cooking, you know what size and type of stove, pans

and utensils you will need. There are lots of things you can cook with one or two pans and minimal kit – check out the recipe section in this book.

3 When choosing a stove for an adventure, think about the type of fuel and how much you will need, and whether it's available en route? Consider the overall weight and volume of the stove pans and fuel for the trip.

CAMPING THROUGH THE SEASONS – TOP TIPS

SPRING

- Springtime weather is notoriously changeable, with versatility being the number one requirement for camping kit and clothing. Expect rain and gales early in the season, with late spring bringing a combination of the two, interspersed with warm days reminiscent of mid-summer.
- Pitch your tent well clear of rivers that may rise quickly after heavy rain or with snowmelt.
- Make sure your tent is robust and waterproof enough to deal with wet and windy weather, but still have sufficient ventilation for those warmer days. If it's been a while since you last went camping, check everything thoroughly before setting out to make sure it's all fully weatherproof and in good working order.
- Pitch carefully and peg out your tent thoroughly.
- Night-time temperatures can drop rapidly, with frost and even ice still possible, so sleeping systems should be sufficient to keep you comfortable.
- Make the most of the tender young leaves of nettle, wild garlic and other edible foraged greens, adding them to soups, stews, curries and pestos.

SUMMER

- Ventilation and breathability are essential for warm-weather camping. Cotton canvas fabrics are more breathable and feel much more pleasant to live in when it's hot.
- Tents with a mesh inner offer the best ventilation. Choosing a tent with an inner

that can pitch on its own enables you to create a bug-free and fairly private space that won't become an oven in the midday sun.

● Pitch in a shady spot if it's practicable to do so, but be aware of falling branches, wildlife and other hazards.

● Consider removing the flysheet of your tent during the day to reduce UV damage to the fabric and increase its useful life.

● Take a tarp, which can be pitched and positioned in a variety of ways, to offer protection from the sun.

● Consider taking a cool box for fresh food, or check campsite facilities for fridge/freezers.

● Protect against insects. Pack a repellent if you're visiting a place where insects are likely to be a problem. Lavender and mint essential oils are effective, as are the DEET-based repellents found in outdoor shops. Keep zips done up, especially on the inner/bedroom tent, to stop unwanted visitors invading.

AUTUMN

● Like spring, autumn is one of the more unpredictable seasons, when versatility and planning are key for happy camping. A warm dry autumn, however, can be the best time of year for camping, when the summer crowds have vanished, the heat of the day is slightly less intense and the sea has had plenty of time to warm up.

● Keep in mind the wind direction when pitching, using all your peg points and making the most of any available shelter.

● Steer clear of rivers that could flood after heavy rain.

● Early autumn is often one of the best times of year for foraging, with apples, plums, berries and nuts providing an abundance of free food from the trees and hedgerows.

WINTER

● Campsites are likely to be muddy, so use a groundsheet protector to keep everything cleaner. Laying a plank, pallet or a few stepping-stones to make a walkway from the entrance to your tent stops regular footfall creating a quagmire, and helps prevent mud from encroaching into your nice clean tent.

● A foam roll mat, placed under your usual sleeping mat, will add warmth and comfort to your sleeping system. Adding a tent carpet, or even a thin rug, on top of your tent groundsheet adds warmth and comfort to your living space, and makes everything feel nicer.

● If you camp in a tent with a single, large internal space such as a bell tent or tipi, adding inner tents to sleep in is much warmer than sleeping in one big, draughty space.

● If electric hook-up is available where you're camping, a small convection heater allows you to quickly, easily and safely warm up the inside of your tent.

● Consider using winter gas mixtures, which are higher in propane and work more effectively at low temperatures. Alternatively, use a liquid fuel stove as these aren't affected by temperature.

● Tents will almost always be damp when you pack away after winter camping trips. Get everything out to dry and air as soon as you can once you're home.

Cooking equipment

Pots and pans

It's perfectly acceptable to take your everyday kitchen saucepans camping but, particularly if you're planning to try out some new methods of outdoor cookery, or need the lightest version possible, there are plenty of camping-specific options on the market. Pans come in a variety of sizes, from single-person mugs to huge multi-person Dutch ovens, and can be made from stainless steel, aluminium, titanium or cast iron. Your choice of material depends on the importance of weight, size, durability and cooking efficiency. Here are some pros and cons of various materials to consider when making your choice:

Caring for cast iron

Cast iron is perfect for outdoor cooking and you'll find it used in Dutch ovens, skillets, pans and kettles. It's ideal for use on open fires or fire pits when you can use the residual heat of the embers to finish off cooking.

Cast-iron cookware either comes unseasoned or preseasoned. If the inside of the pan is black, it's likely already seasoned. If it's grey, it will need seasoning before use. Seasoning and subsequent use creates a coating on the pan called a patina. This acts as a natural, protective non-stick and must be maintained through regular use in order to keep the pan working at its best. It sounds like a faff, but it's a routine you'll soon get used to and it's honestly worth it.

If your pan hasn't been seasoned, or it hasn't been used recently and has formed

Type	Pros	Cons
Stainless steel	Very durable although may be damaged by metal utensils, average price, cooks evenly.	Lower heat conduction than aluminium or titanium. Heavy.
Aluminium	Lighter than steel, usually good value and reasonably durable. High conductivity means rapid heating and cooling.	Easily damaged by metal utensils. Some health concerns with regular use.
Titanium	Strong, lightweight, high conductivity so heats up and cools down quickly. Ideal for fast-and-light adventures.	Expensive. Hard not to burn food so best for boiling water to be added to food rather than cooking directly.
Cast iron	Strong, durable, stable and brilliant to cook in once seasoned.	Very heavy and takes a while to heat up – best for vehicle camping and base camp where weight and fuel aren't an issue. Requires seasoning and care to keep it performing at its best.

a thin layer of rust, you'll need to perform an initial seasoning before using it.

1   Wash the pan thoroughly, using a lightly abrasive sponge if you need to remove any rust – you can use soap at this point if you wish, but after this soap shouldn't go near your cast iron.
2   Dry the pan thoroughly.
3   Add a small amount of oil – use an oil with a high smoke point – and, using a piece of kitchen paper towel, rub it all over the pan.
4   Place the pan upside down in a domestic oven and bake it at 200°C (400°F) for an hour, then turn the oven off, leaving the pan inside to cool slowly.

Having seasoned your pan, keep it in good condition by using it regularly – you'll find the natural non-stick patina improves gradually over time. After each use, rather than washing your pan with soap and water, rinse with water and wipe. If it needs a more thorough cleaning, add some water and heat to a boil, which allows any stuck-on food to be removed easily, then dry thoroughly and wipe with a little oil to finish.

▲ Making coffee using an MSR Whisperlite multi-fuel stove

How to cook in a Dutch oven

Once you get to know your Dutch oven, it'll feel like a lifelong friend. First, though, we need to run through a few icebreakers to get you acquainted and on your way.

1   Season your oven if it needs seasoning. Many Dutch ovens come preseasoned – if your pan has a black finish, it's probably been preseasoned. If not, you'll need to season it as described for cast iron on page 169. Avoid cooking acidic foods like tomatoes and fruit in your Dutch oven for the first few times you use it after its first seasoning as these may damage the patina that is still in its early stages of forming. Once the pan has been used several times, the patina will be robust enough to withstand any recipe.

2   Dutch ovens can be used to cook on a wood fire that has burned down to its last glowing embers, or on charcoal briquettes. We prefer briquettes as they produce less smoke and it's easier to maintain a constant temperature or alter the temperature when required by adding or removing briquettes from the base and/or lid.

3   If you're using briquettes, a chimney starter is a great investment, and not an expensive one. These have a space in the base for a small fire made from paper, card or kindling and then a shelf for the briquettes above. A chimney starter allows you to preheat briquettes in the quantity you require them and then create the base on which to set your Dutch oven. More briquettes can easily be heated as required.

The Dutch oven process – from heating briquettes in a chimney starter to baking bread

How to calculate the number of briquettes to use with your Dutch oven

Depending on the size of your Dutch oven (measured in inches) and the heat you want to cook at, there's a simple formula you can use to work out the number of briquettes you'll need. Taking the diameter of your Dutch oven in inches and doubling it will give you the number of briquettes to use in order to reach a temperature of about 180°C (350°F) with roughly two-thirds of the briquettes on top and one-third underneath. For 8in Dutch ovens, adding or removing one briquette increases or decreases the temperature by about 4°C (25°F). For 10in and larger Dutch ovens, adding or removing two briquettes increases or decreases the temperature by about 4°C (25°F). Alternatively, check the following table.

TEMPERATURE/NUMBER OF BRIQUETTES FOR DIFFERENT DUTCH OVEN SIZES

	Oven size	Temperature					
		160°C (325°F)	180°C (350°F)	190°C (375°F)	200°C (400°F)	220°C (425°F)	230°C (450°F)
#briquettes	8"	15	16	17	18	19	20
	TOP	10	11	11	12	13	14
	BOTTOM	5	5	6	6	6	6
	10"	19	21	23	25	27	29
	TOP	13	14	16	17	18	19
	BOTTOM	6	7	7	8	9	10
	12"	23	25	27	29	31	33
	TOP	16	17	18	19	21	22
	BOTTOM	7	8	9	10	10	11
	14"	30	32	34	36	38	40
	TOP	20	21	22	24	25	26
	BOTTOM	10	11	12	12	13	14

Kettles and coffee

Camping kettles are available in a range of materials, from heavy-bottomed cast iron to super-lightweight titanium, depending on your preference. They're a great choice for open-air cooking as the shape and closed top make them more efficient for boiling water than a pan, and easier to pour. Aside from the more traditional kettle designs, stove systems such as the Jetboil, MSR Reactor and Primus Lite boil water rapidly and efficiently and can be a great choice for lightweight camping trips –

▲ The daily grind: coffee beans + hand grinder + percolator + gas stove = coffee

more on these in our 'stoves' section above.

Coffee is an important part of our day, perhaps even more so when we're camping. There's something about the routine, lengthened by being outside and often far from the convenience of electric hook-up, that makes that first coffee of the day particularly special. But how do you make your coffee? A camping kettle works perfectly for cafetière/French press and pour-over methods. Stove-top percolators such as Bialetti's Moka Express are great for smaller camping stoves, producing a more espresso-like end result. There are larger percolators designed specifically for camping, such as the Petromax 28-cup model, which are useful for making larger quantities of coffee without compromising on the quality of your brew. Or, for more versatility, Snow Peak's Field Coffee Master combines a percolator and pour-over so you can go for whichever suits your morning best. Another popular camping coffee-maker is the AeroPress, which consists of two plastic tubes, one of which fits inside the other to create a pressurised press. Although they're light, portable and produce a smooth, grit-free end result thanks to the filter paper, you'll need to boil your water in a separate container such as a kettle or Jetboil. And there's also the plastic, which some users don't like.

Ultimately, how we all like to make and drink our coffee is personal preference, but there's no reason to compromise just because you're camping – great coffee is possible pretty much anywhere!

There's no reason to compromise just because you're camping – great coffee is possible pretty much anywhere!

Utensils

A decent set of utensils makes food prep easier and more enjoyable – camping shouldn't mean battling with blunt knives or using tent pegs as bottle openers.

If you're travelling very light, then one spoon per person and a good penknife may be all you need. For anything else, we always take a couple of wooden spoons, a spatula (without which omelettes and pancakes are an absolute nightmare), vegetable peeler, bottle and can opener, flat cheese grater, serving spoon and a big chef's knife. We also take a chopping board, which makes slicing and chopping much easier. It's also helpful to take lightweight weighing scales and/or measuring cups, for measuring ingredients for recipes such as pancakes and cookies.

If space isn't an issue, everyday kitchen kit works perfectly, but several brands make camping-specific versions that save on space, weight or add safety features such as a sheath to blades for portable protection. The Opinel Nomad set includes a 12cm (4¾in) serrated folding knife, brilliant for bread or veg chopping, a small peeler, a small blade and a corkscrew. The three knives are wrapped up in a cloth with a small chopping board. Primus also makes a great chef's set including a knife, wooden spoons and chopping board.

Keep all your kitchen kit together and organised using a chef roll or camping-specific version, such as the Kelty Camp

Heating water and melting snow

HEATING WATER FOR FOOD and drink is the most basic requirement of camp cooking. On some trips it might be all you need to do if you're eating dehydrated food, with the added benefit of never having to wash a pan.

If you're at a campsite with electric hook-up you can use a low-energy camp kettle, while on an open fire or fire pit, a steel or cast-iron kettle can work well. But for the most part, to boil water efficiently you'll need some kind of stove. Stove-top kettles are more efficient and easier to pour from than pans, so use one if space and weight allow. Otherwise, an integrated stove system is the quickest

– ideal for single-night stopovers, rapid early morning coffees and making hot drinks at the car when out adventuring.

Melting snow or ice for water always uses lots of fuel, but sometimes there is no other option. It works best if you have some water in the pan to start with to get the melting going. Bear in mind that as snow melts it significantly reduces in volume, so make sure you have a good supply of clean snow near the stove and keep adding it as you go until you have enough water. To avoid your hard-won water refreezing, keep water bottles in the inside pocket of your jacket or inside your sleeping bag overnight.

Galley, which has a range of pockets and pouches and can hang up for easy access.

Cutlery and crockery

Camping plates, bowls, mugs, cutlery and even champagne flutes are widely available. But they're often made of plastic and as a result are not particularly pleasant to use. On the upside, they're lightweight, packable, and don't easily break. After years of trying various options, we've concluded that, for car camping at least, taking along a ceramic pasta bowl each works really well. The shape of these bowls means they're extremely versatile, good for everything from porridge for breakfast and soup for lunch to pasta for supper. They're also pretty chunky and therefore robust, and so far, we haven't had any breakages. For cutlery, either pack your usual set or invest in one of the combination forks and spoons (sporks and foons), which sometimes also include a knife incorporated into the fork.

A big, heavy pasta bowl and full set of cutlery might work perfectly for family car camping trips, but for solo, lightweight adventures things can look quite different. Options gradually get smaller, lighter and more combined until at the very least you'll take a titanium mug that doubles as a pan and bowl, with a lightweight spork (or foon) for stirring and eating.

Other useful items

For car camping or longer expeditions for which weight isn't an issue, remember to take a few tea towels and dish cloths with you. It's also very useful to have clingfilm, baking parchment and aluminium foil, and some empty containers for storing leftovers or containing sandwiches or other foods for a day away from camp. A couple of bags for life are invaluable for trips to the shops, as well as for packing-up time.

Food

Keeping cool

If you're away for more than a couple of nights, it's useful to be able to keep perishables cold. Some campsites have a shared fridge, but this is quite rare and never feels like an ideal solution. There are three options that we think work well for camping, depending on the length of the trip and your power options.

(A quick note on staying cool: unlike domestic versions, even plug-in camping fridges and coolers only cool the contents by a certain number of degrees compared with the ambient temperature, rather than to a specific temperature.)

Cool boxes and cool bags

These are simply insulated boxes or bags that will keep whatever is inside them cold (or hot) for longer. They come in a huge range of different shapes and sizes, from supermarket cool bags designed to keep your shopping cold on the journey home to backcountry cool boxes that, if well packed, will keep things frozen for several days.

Cool boxes are best for camping as they protect food from being squashed as well as keeping it cold. They work by insulating already cold things against heat loss, so you'll need to start out with some frozen items to keep everything cold for longer. Freeze blocks are good, and many campsites offer the ability to refreeze these during your stay. We'll often pack a couple of bags of frozen fruit and vegetables in alongside anything that needs keeping cool, which is usually effective for a couple of days. And by the time the frozen produce is defrosted, we're ready to use it for stews and crumbles.

Larger cool boxes often come with wheels and a handle as they can be very heavy when full. A drain plug at the bottom is also handy, especially if you plan to use loose ice.

Plug-in coolers

Plug-in coolers are insulated cool boxes with a powered lid that will typically cool the contents to about 18°C (64°F) lower than the outside temperature. They can normally run off the 12V socket in your car, so you can keep the contents cool on the journey, then plug them into the electric hook-up at the campsite. If you don't have hook-up, they still work as an insulated cool box, keeping everything cold for a few hours until you next find a power source. As with non-powered versions, adding freeze blocks or frozen food helps keep everything cold.

Plug-in coolers usually have a fan to circulate cool air, so they make a bit of noise, which is worth considering at night. They also need some air space around them to work effectively.

Camping fridges

These are mini versions of a proper fridge, so provided that they're connected to a reliable power source, they will keep food cold indefinitely. Some even have separate cold and frozen compartments like a domestic fridge. They are considerably more expensive than plug-in coolers and tend to be a bit bigger and heavier, so they're best for longer stays in one place. Camping fridges can be powered via an electric hook-up, power bank or battery system. If you're using a power bank or battery, bear in mind that fridges are on all the time so you will need enough stored power to last between charges. Gas-powered fridges are also available, which can be a good option if you don't have electric hook-up.

Fridges normally have a thermostat and will work to cool the interior to a specified temperature. It will take a lot more power to cool a fridge in a hot place than a cold place so always keep them in a cool and shaded spot.

Foraging

Camping in wild places gives you access to nature's larder. With a few basic rules, you can forage easily and safely, adding top-quality fresh ingredients to your meals or a handy snack to your travels. As much of the best, widely available foraging involves berries and fungi, both of which can be deadly if you get the identification wrong, careful and knowledgeable foraging is essential. A big disclaimer here: never eat anything unless you're 100 per cent sure what it is. As far as we're concerned this should be a warning on packaged foods as well as foraged ones. Alongside safety for the forager is safety for the foraged: only ever pick what is growing abundantly, never pick protected or rare species, and cause as little damage as possible.

Top foods for fun, safe foraging

● Wild blackberries and raspberries – easily recognisable and abundant in many countries, blackberries (brambles) and raspberries are delicious and provide freshness, sugars, protein and other essential nutrients such as vitamin C and polyphenols. They can be found in hedgerows and woodland and are easily identifiable by their shape, colour and sweet taste.

● Bilberries – another easily recognisable, delicious and nutritious berry, bilberry bushes often grow thickly on woodland and forest floors, as well as moorland and mountainside. In the summer months, the tiny indigo fruits are easy to pick and they're a great trail snack to graze on as you go. They're also known as whortleberries, myrtle berries and blueberries, among other names. Don't use the rake-like berry pickers as, while they might save you a bit of time, they're both indiscriminate and damaging.

● Nuts – in the autumn, freshly picked nuts are a perfect foraged treat – as long as you have something to crack them with. Where we live in south-west Britain, hazelnuts and walnuts are abundant in the autumn.

● Wild garlic – during the spring, many woodlands glow with the vibrant colour and heady aroma of wild garlic. The leaves are a great addition to soups, curries, stews and salads, while the flowers are a tasty nibble and a pretty garnish.

● Fungi – for those who know exactly what they're picking, fungi offer a vast array of tasty, protein-rich, easily forageable food. Get it wrong, however, and the consequences can be extremely serious, and even fatal. If you're not an expert and you'd like to forage for fungi, book on to a course, hire an expert, or go somewhere like France where you can take your pickings into a pharmacy to check they're safe to eat.

Local food

One of the best things about travel is immersion in a new culture, and a new cuisine. Be open to trying new things, asking expert locals about what's good and safe to eat, trying locally produced and artisan foods and new ways of preparing and cooking food. We've variously returned from England's Peak District with a taste for Derbyshire oat cakes (nothing like the Scottish ones!), from Beaufortain in the French Alps with a craving for the local Beaufort cheese, and from Sweden keen to learn how to cook on a forest pan.

Food for multi-day adventures

When you're heading out into wilder areas where food isn't readily available – for example on a multi-day backpacking, bikepacking or canoe camping trip (lots more on these in Chapter 5) – you'll need to carefully plan out the food to take. By working out what you'll need, and want, for breakfast, lunch and supper plus snacks for each day of your trip, you'll avoid the perils of packing too little, running out of food and having a very uncomfortable and hungry time. It sounds obvious, but we've all done it!

When space is at a premium, which it usually is on multi-day adventures, you'll only be able to take the minimum with you, so every item must count. To cook on, you'll need a lightweight and packable camping stove plus gas or your choice of fuel, as well as a source of ignition (and, of course, a back-up source of ignition).

For food prep and eating, you'll need a small pan that doubles as a bowl, and a mug, spoon and penknife.

Food that is easy to cook – often by simply adding it to boiling water and stirring – while also being satisfying and filling is key. Some of our favourites include:

- Fresh food for the first couple of days – apples, oranges and cucumbers are all good ways to carry extra liquid as well as adding some much-needed freshness and crunch to your diet.
- Quick-cook filled fresh pasta – a hearty meal that takes three minutes to cook in boiling water, packs plenty of calories and is available in a range of flavours.
- Packet noodles, pasta and dried potato flakes (go for one made with 100 per cent potato as this is much nicer than the well-known brands packed with nasty additives) – add stock to the boiling water to add flavour and electrolytes.
- Instant stuffing mix – just add boiling water for a quick and satisfying herby hit.
- Energy-rich breakfasts such as porridge and muesli – add powdered dairy or plant milk and some dried fruit for an instant, just-add-water breakfast.
- Packets of custard powder or other instant dessert.
- Good-quality packet meals – available ready to empty into a pan and heat through or dehydrated so you need to add water. It's tempting to simply order a load of the packet meals specifically marketed for outdoor adventure use but, if you're choosing the ready-to-heat kind, you'll often find far tastier options in your local supermarket at a fraction of the price. Even the top-of-the-range organic versions usually work out cheaper, and they taste much, much nicer.
- Tea/coffee bags, hot chocolate, hydration tablets.

Cooking outdoors

Travelling fast-and-light presents an intriguing challenge when it comes to preparing and cooking meals: how to get the most calories for the least weight and fuel. However, one of the great joys of camping when you have the luxury of space – both while travelling and once you've made camp – is the ability to cook outdoors with the time, equipment and ingredients you need to conjure up some truly special dishes.

With a bit of imagination and inventiveness, it's amazing what you can create using a camping stove, a Dutch oven (also known as a camp oven) or an open fire/fire pit. If you're after some inspiration, start by thinking about your favourite meals at home – how could they be customised to suit camp cooking? Then there's a wealth of incredible books and websites dedicated to outdoor cooking – you'll find some of our favourites listed in the Resources section of this book.

Practising outdoor cooking is a lot of fun and adds an adventurous feel to a weekday night. We regularly head out to the garden to cook and eat al fresco, even when we're not camping. There's something about outdoor cooking that makes it a more exciting, sociable affair – kids and guests always love to get involved, too. As long as it's dry and not too windy, cooking outdoors is practical and enjoyable all year round. We find it a perfect way to reconnect with the changing seasons, brightening up dark winter evenings and making the most of the long, light summer ones.

◄ Getting our Biolite stove ready to cook on and charging the phone at the same time

Recipes

BREAKFAST/BRUNCH

When we're away camping, we're always ravenous at breakfast time. Perhaps it's all the extra exercise and fresh air, or the smells wafting over as other campers cook up delicious things, or the excitement about what to make and how to make it... Most probably, it's all three. Breakfast can be as quick and simple or as gourmet as you choose. If we're wild camping, we'll often take a flapjack each for a delicious, filling and easy breakfast. But when we're fully set up on a campsite, we take any opportunity to get creative with ingredients, kit and techniques, cooking up more elaborate brunches to be savoured late morning with plenty of coffee. Here are some of our favourite tried-and-tested best breakfast and brunch recipes for camping.

Fast-and-light pancakes

PANCAKES ARE ALWAYS a popular camping breakfast, but you need to get the mix, cooking set-up and technique right, which can take a little practice. It's well worth the effort though.

The first thing to prepare is the basic dry mix for the batter. This can be weighed out at home, mixed well and then stored in an airtight container ready for use. When you're ready to cook your pancakes, all you need to do is add liquid and stir. These can be made vegan and/or gluten free, as directed in the tips opposite.

SERVES
4

Ingredients

300g (11oz) self-raising flour
1 tbsp sugar – vanilla sugar
    works particularly well
40g (1½oz) milk powder
A pinch of salt
400ml (13½fl oz) water
Butter or oil for cooking
Toppings, such as maple
    syrup and sliced banana,
    chocolate hazelnut spread
    or nut butter and sliced
    banana, jam, fruit compote
    – apple and cinnamon,
    dried fruit or foraged berries
    are all good – or the classic
    lemon and sugar

Equipment

Weighing scales
Sealable container
Spoon
Whisk
Small frying pan
Camping stove
Spatula

Method

1 Before leaving home, weigh out and combine all the dry ingredients in a clean, dry, sealable container. Tupperware boxes and large jam jars work well. Mix to combine and put the lid on firmly.

2 When you're ready to make your pancakes, gradually add the water to your dry ingredients in the container or jar, mixing vigorously as you go – use a whisk if you have one. Once you have a smooth batter, set it aside to rest for a few minutes.

3 Put your frying pan on a medium heat and add a pat of butter or a drizzle/spray of oil. Once the pan is hot, pour in enough of the batter to thinly coat the base of the pan, tilting it gently to ensure a good coverage.

4 Allow the pancake to cook. Once small holes start to form on the surface and the edges start to crisp, flip it over with a spatula and cook on the other side. Your pancake should be a golden colour when it's done.

5 Stack your pancakes somewhere warm or serve each one to your hungry campers as you go.

6 Liberally add toppings of your choice. NB: these toppings also work brilliantly on porridge…

TOP
TIP

ADAPTING
THE RECIPE

- To make gluten-free pancakes, replace the flour with a mix of oat and chestnut flours and add 1 tsp baking powder.
- For a high-protein version, use whey powder instead of milk powder – enough to make 400ml (13½fl oz) milk.
- To make vegan pancakes, use powdered plant milk – there are several available, including coconut, oat and almond.

Adventure porridge

PORRIDGE HAS TO BE the ultimate camping breakfast – stuffed full of slow-release energy, warm and satisfying, customisable to suit almost every taste and dietary need. Oats are naturally gluten free but are often processed in factories that also handle gluten, so if you need gluten-free ones look out for oats specifically labelled as such. Porridge is good made just with water – traditionally also with a small pinch of salt. We usually use half-and-half water and milk, but you can also make it with all milk if you prefer. Plant milks work really well in porridge, and often fare better out of the fridge than dairy. Powdered plant or dairy milk, which you can even premix with your oats, is a great way to save weight while adding some extra nutrients to your breakfast.

Good porridge toppings include all those suggested for pancakes but extend well beyond these as you're serving it in a bowl and eating it with a spoon – nuts, seeds, grated or stewed apple with cinnamon and raisins, and a sprinkling of dark sugar are all favourites. For summer camping, a handful of foraged blackberries, raspberries and/or bilberries and a drizzle of maple syrup is hard to beat.

The measure is generally a cup, meaning you don't need to weigh the oats. Allow about half a measuring cup of oats per person, then calculate how much liquid you need.

SERVES 4

Ingredients

2 mugs of oats (approx. 100g per person) – we like a mix of porridge and jumbo oats
4 mugs of liquid – milk/plant milk, water or half-and-half
Your choice of toppings

Equipment

Measuring cup
Saucepan
Camping stove
Wooden spoon

Method

Add your measure of oats and twice the volume of liquid to the pan. Cook slowly until thick and creamy, stirring often. Serve in a bowl with toppings of your choice.

French toast

SERVING UP SOME of the same experience as pancakes, but with a lot less risk for the camping chef, French toast (or eggy bread if you're under ten) is another great way to start the day. It's also brilliant for using up bread that's going a bit dry – in fact, slightly stale bread works best for this recipe as it holds together better.

French toast is very versatile, pairing well with sweet or savoury flavours – or both if the inclination takes you. Sizzled in lightly salted butter in a cast-iron pan over a rocket stove or other heat source and then doused generously in maple syrup, this is hands-down one of the best breakfasts we can think of. But once you have the basics you can get as creative as you wish – try French toast as the base for a cooked breakfast topped with mushrooms, tomatoes and beans; USA-style with maple syrup and crispy bacon; or cut into strips as finger food for smaller children, with a dip of their choice.

SERVES
2

Ingredients

2 thick slices of bread
2 free-range eggs
A pinch of salt
A splash of milk
Butter or oil for cooking
Toppings of your choice

Equipment

Bread knife and chopping
   board
Medium-sized bowl
Whisk or fork
Well-seasoned cast-iron
   frying pan or skillet
Stove with a good strong
   flame – we love our rocket
   stove for this dish
Spatula

Method

1 Cut the bread into thick, chunky slices, then cut each slice into two or three equal pieces – these can be rectangles or triangles, whatever you like the look of. You can leave the slices of bread whole if you're using a larger pan, but we find smaller pieces soak up the egg mixture more quickly and are easier to manoeuvre around the pan while cooking.

2 Break the eggs into a medium-sized bowl, add a splash of milk and a pinch of salt and mix well.

3 Add the bread to the egg mixture and allow it to soak for a couple of minutes, turning it over to ensure it's completely coated.

4 Place the frying pan or skillet on top your flame and add a pat of butter or a splash of oil. Once the butter has melted and started to foam or the oil is sizzling, carefully transfer the eggy bread, one piece at a time, to the pan. Sizzle on one side, then turn over to cook the other. Chunkier pieces may need to be turned on to their edges to cook these too.

5 Once the bread is golden brown all over, remove from the pan and serve. It's fantastic just as it is or add your choice of toppings.

One-pan brunch

DRAWING ITS INSPIRATION from France and Spain, this satisfying brunch dish lies somewhere between an omelette and a tortilla. Using just one pan, it's perfect for cooking on a camping stove (along with minimal washing-up), brilliantly customisable to suit a range of tastes, and any leftovers are delicious cold the following day. It works just as well for lunch or supper, too – add some cubed potato along with your onions at the start and fry gently until these are soft for a more substantial meal that's also great cut into chunky slices to take out on a walk or day trip.

SERVES 3-4

Ingredients

Your choice of additions – peeled and diced onions, wiped and sliced mushrooms, sliced sausage/veggie sausage, diced bacon, deseeded and diced bell peppers, sun-dried or sliced cherry tomatoes, and cubed preboiled potatoes all work well

6 free-range eggs
Salt and pepper, to taste
Oil for cooking

Equipment

Knife and chopping board
Medium-sized bowl
Well-seasoned cast-iron frying pan or skillet
Single-burner stove, ideally one with variable heat
Spatula or wooden spoon
Fork
Plate

Method

1 Prepare your additional ingredients.
2 Crack the eggs into a bowl, add seasoning and beat together.
3 Add a little oil to your frying pan or skillet and heat over a medium flame.
4 Add the onions, if using, and fry gently until soft. If you're using sausage or bacon, add this now and make sure it's cooked through. Then add the remaining additions and cook for a few more minutes.
5 Drain any excess oil and spread the cooked ingredients out around the pan.
6 Turn the flame down to a low/medium heat and add the eggs, tilting the pan to fill any spaces. Use a fork to gently move the egg around as it cooks.
7 Once the bottom of your omelette is cooked, you'll need to cook the top. To do this, you can either pop your pan under a grill if you have one or use the plate method. Place a plate over the top of the frying pan and quickly turn both over so that the omelette is now on the plate. Carefully slide it back into the pan to finish cooking.
8 Cut into wedges and serve.

Cowgirl beans

DISHES OF PORK AND BEANS – often known as cowboy beans or chuckwagon beans – are popular in south-western USA. Recipes vary widely, but the key ingredients of beans, pork and warming, substantial flavours are always there. Some versions suggest the addition of coffee, which adds a subtle bitterness, and is said to originate from cowboys using their leftover coffee water to add liquid to the dish when fresh water was hard to come by.

This is one of those dishes that lends itself well to experimentation – it can be made with minced (ground) beef, pork sausages, smoked bacon and/or the traditional ham hock, or as an equally satisfying vegan dish. Whichever you prefer, it's perfect for camping trips when the combination of filling, protein-rich beans, a good kick of chilli and some extra campfire smoke is just what's needed after a long day of adventures.

For this vegan version, we use a three-bean mix. Adzuki and black beans create the background texture you'd otherwise get from minced beef, while butter beans add contrast and nuttiness. We also use veggie sausages, cut into chunky pieces, which take on the delicious smokiness of the sauce.

SERVES 6

Ingredients

Oil for cooking
6 sausages of your choice
1 large onion, peeled and chopped
1 tsp chipotle paste (or more/less depending on how spicy you like it)
2–3 garlic cloves, peeled and chopped
400g (14oz) can passata or tinned chopped tomatoes
1 tbsp good-quality barbecue sauce
1 rosemary sprig
3 x 400g (14oz) cans beans, drained – black, adzuki, borlotti, pinto, haricot butter or mixed beans all work well

Salt and pepper, to taste
Toppings, such as pickled jalapeño chillies, grated cheese, sour cream and sliced avocado
Crusty bread or jacket potatoes (see pages 194 and 198), to serve

Equipment

Large, fairly deep-sided frying pan
Camping stove with a large base to ensure cooking right to the edges of the frying pan. Also works well on a fire pit or rocket stove
Knife and chopping board
Spatula or wooden spoon

Method

1   Add a splash of oil to your frying pan and place over a medium flame. If using an open flame such as a rocket stove or fire pit, you may need to take the pan off the heat from time to time so the ingredients don't burn.

2   If you're using meat sausages, cook these first, then set them aside and drain any excess fat.

3   Add the chopped onion to the pan and fry for a few minutes, until soft. Add the sausages and, unless pre-cooked, cook for a few minutes until browned, then push

to one side. Add the chipotle paste and garlic and cook for a further minute, then add the passata or chopped tomatoes, a splash of water (rinse out the passata/tomato jar or tin), the barbecue sauce and the rosemary sprig. Stir well and leave to bubble for a few minutes.

4 Add the beans and stir well, then allow to simmer for 15 minutes, stirring regularly, until thickened. Remove the rosemary and season to taste.

5 Serve in big bowls with toppings of your choice and a side of crusty bread or jacket potatoes (see page 194).

Shakshuka

HAILING FROM MAGHREB – north-west Africa – shakshuka is a popular breakfast or anytime dish. Simple, healthy, comforting and, best of all, made in one pan, shakshuka is one of our outdoor cooking staples. It's endlessly customisable, depending on what you like and what you have to hand – different versions are found across the Maghrebi region. Beans, mushrooms, sliced sausages, courgettes, boiled potatoes, olives, and spices such as ground cumin and coriander, harissa, cayenne pepper and paprika all pair well with the basic flavours. Feta-style cheese can also be crumbled over the top before serving.

SERVES 4

Ingredients

1 tbsp olive oil or other cooking oil

1 large or 2 small red onions, peeled and chopped

1 red and 1 yellow bell pepper, deseeded and sliced

1 red chilli, deseeded and finely chopped, or 1 tsp dried chilli flakes

2 garlic cloves, peeled and chopped

1 tsp smoked paprika

1 tsp ground cumin

1 tsp ground coriander

Salt and pepper to taste

2 x 400g (14oz) cans tinned cherry tomatoes

1 tsp sugar or 2 tsp tomato ketchup

4 free-range eggs

Scattering of fresh coriander leaves, to garnish

Crusty bread, (see page 198) to serve

Equipment

Medium-large cast-iron frying pan with a lid – if there's no lid then a sheet of aluminium foil works well

Camping stove

Knife and chopping board

Wooden spoon

Mug (optional)

Method

1   Heat the oil in the frying pan over a medium heat, add the onions and cook until softened. Add the bell peppers and cook for about five minutes, then add the chilli, garlic and spices and cook for a few more minutes until everything is soft.

2   Stir in the tomatoes and sugar or ketchup, then simmer for around ten minutes, until thickened.

3   Using the back of a spoon, make four hollows in the tomato and pepper mixture, then carefully crack an egg into each one. If you prefer, you can crack the eggs one at a time into a mug and pour each one into the sauce – this is a great way to avoid broken yolks and pieces of shell in the food.

4   Put a lid on the pan or cover with a piece of foil. Cook over a medium-low heat until the eggs are done to your liking. Scatter with the fresh coriander leaves and serve with crusty bread.

COOKING JACKET POTATOES

TOP TIP

Jacket potatoes are fantastic camping food – warming, satisfying and endlessly customisable. They can be cooked in a Dutch oven or wriggled into the glowing coals or embers of an open fire. To cook jacket potatoes, prick each potato several times with a fork. Rub with butter or oil, plus salt and pepper if desired, then double wrap in aluminum foil and place in the Dutch oven with the lid on, or into a pile of glowing coals/embers.

Cook until crisp on the outside and soft inside – give them a quick squeeze to check they're done. Larger potatoes will take considerably longer to cook than small ones but, depending on their size, they'll usually cook in around an hour.

▲ MSR by Bard Basberg

MAIN MEALS AND LIGHT BITES

Sitting down to a hearty main meal after a good day's adventuring offers a wonderful time to rest, refuel, share stories and make plans. From simple pasta dishes that even the pickiest tween will love, to more elaborate richly spiced curries, there's a vast scope for experimenting with a range of different techniques and some carefully chosen camp-cooking equipment. Baking bread and cooking pizzas wasn't something we associated with camping until we discovered the magic of the Dutch oven, but now even these make a regular and endlessly popular appearance on our camping menu. A sizeable loaf is brilliantly versatile, too – perfect for sandwiches, French toast (*see page 186*), and mopping up sauces.

Campfire toasties

TOASTED SANDWICHES are perfect campfire food, sealing a vast array of delicious fillings inside a crisp bread shell to create a hand-held portable meal. For the best results, you will need to invest in a campfire toastie-maker, of which there are many available on the market. Long-handled cast-iron versions are particularly good if you'll be making your panini over an open fire. Most will work well nestled in the glowing coals or embers of a fire – if you're using a Dutch oven to make a soup or stew, you can utilise the fire underneath to make toasted sandwiches as an accompaniment. Many models also work well on a stove top, so you can toast panini at home using a gas or electric hob, range cooker or even the top of a wood burner.

The best toastie fillings:

- **Cheese**. The classic toastie filler, cheese melts beautifully when heated, resulting in that gloriously gooey centre. Try a mature cheddar paired with sliced onion for sweetness and crunch, or add chutney or pickle for tang and texture. Simply sliced or grated gruyere conjures up the popular Alpine panini. Mozzarella works perfectly with pesto and sliced tomatoes. Or pair a ripe brie or camembert with cranberry sauce. Vegan cheeses work well in all of the above, too.
- **Chocolate**. Toasties also make great puddings, and chocolate, oozy and melting, is hard to beat. Pair with sliced banana, salted caramel sauce, peanut butter or thinly sliced pear for a heavenly sweet treat. Chunks of well-known chocolate bars (those with caramel and nutty interiors work best) also make for an easy, tasty toastie.

SAVOIE FRANCE

TOP TIP

Place your fillings towards the centre of your slice of bread, leaving enough of a margin around the edge for the toastie maker to create a seal to stop your fillings escaping.

Dutch oven bread

WE WERE AMAZED the first time we tried baking a loaf in our Dutch oven. We made the dough and let it prove, then shaped it, proved it again and, after sprinkling the base of the oven with some flour, popped the loaf in, made some cuts into the top to control the rise, and closed the lid, sitting the Dutch oven on a bed of hot briquettes and adding a few more to the top. Some 45 minutes later, we tentatively opened the lid (using a pot lifter – never touch a Dutch oven lid with your hands unless you're absolutely certain it's cool) and couldn't believe our eyes. A perfect loaf, looking very much like it had just been crafted in an artisan bakery.

Since that moment of revelation, we've used our Dutch oven whenever it's possible to do so – that is, whenever there's a brief dry spell between the rain showers. If you're considering investing in one, we'd thoroughly recommend it, along with some great books on Dutch oven cooking, which we've included in the Resources section of this book. For now, here's the recipe that created our first ever loaf, and which we still use today. The dry ingredients (except the yeast) can be premixed at home, so you don't need to weigh them out, or just use half a standard 1kg (2.2lb) bag of bread flour – you can use white, wholemeal, granary, spelt or any other flour suitable for breadmaking. The method involves mixing, kneading and proving the dough in the same large bowl so it's also low on mess. If you do your kneading one-handed you can even keep a hand dough-free. The dough is perfect for bread rolls, pizzas and flatbreads, too.

Ingredients

500g (1.1lb) bread flour
1 tsp quick yeast
1 tsp salt
1 tbsp olive oil
300ml (10fl oz) water, ideally lukewarm
Optional: 1 tsp honey or sugar – omit this if
you're using the dough for pizzas or flatbreads

Equipment

Large bowl
Cover for the bowl, such as a silicone lid,
clingfilm or a damp tea towel
Charcoal briquettes for cooking at 180–200°C
(350–400°F) – see table on page 180
Starter chimney
Dutch oven, preferably with a trivet placed
in the base
Sharp knife

Method

1   Put the flour and yeast into the large
bowl.
2   Add the salt (keeping it away from the
yeast, as it can kill it), oil, water and
honey/sugar (if using) and mix together
using one hand.
3   Knead the dough in the bowl, using one
hand to push, pull and stretch it. Allow
a good 10–15 minutes for a thorough
working, until the dough is soft and
elastic – it should feel nice and pliable
but not sticky. If your dough feels too
firm, add a little more water. If it feels too
sticky, add a little more flour. You'll know
when the balance is just right.
4   Cover the bowl and place it somewhere
warm if you can. Leave it for about an
hour (it might need more if conditions
are cooler) until it has doubled in size.

5   If you want to, you can knead and prove
the dough for a second time, which will
give the bread an optimal texture, but
otherwise it works perfectly well as it is.
6   While the dough is proving, heat your
charcoal briquettes in the starter chimney
and arrange the layer going underneath
the Dutch oven. Set the oven on the
briquettes.
7   Shape the dough into a round loaf,
lightly flouring the underneath to prevent
sticking, and place it carefully into the
oven. Slash the top with your sharpest
knife.
8   Put on the lid and add briquettes to
the top. Cook for about 45 minutes,
until browned all over, then carefully
remove from the Dutch oven, leave
to cool slightly and enjoy.

Pizza

PIZZA IS ALWAYS popular – perfect finger food that's endlessly customisable and at its best when it's simple. Pizzas are a great option if you're camping with kids, being something they're familiar with when other camping foods can seem quite different from ones they're used to at home.

We've tried a few different ways of making pizzas outdoors. The easiest is definitely our pizza oven, which, if you like pizza and cooking outdoors, is a great investment and rapidly pays for itself compared with going out for pizza. It's proved hugely popular, whether we're having a family pizza night in the garden or a party with friends. Modern home pizza ovens are portable, efficient and effective, and they're available in wood, gas or multi-fuel options. As well as cooking pizzas, they're great for flatbreads; roasting veg such as bell peppers, tomatoes and onions; grilling meat and fish; and even making skillet cookies.

The second method we use for cooking pizzas while camping is the Dutch oven – see page 178 for general instructions on Dutch oven cooking, and below. You could also use a reflector oven or simply cook the pizza in a frying pan.

Ingredients

A ball of proved bread dough per person
Passata
Grated cheese and/or mozzarella
Toppings of your choice, such as slices of mushrooms, olives, bell peppers, ham, sausages, onions or whatever else you like

Equipment

Knife and chopping board
Spoon
Pizza oven, Dutch oven or reflector oven
Frying pan, if using a reflector oven or cooking the pizza in the pan over a flame

[200]

Methods

- To make a **Dutch oven** pizza, make a basic bread dough as detailed on page 199 and tear off a portion the right size to fill the base of the pan. Shape this into a round using your hands (or you could use a water or wine bottle as a makeshift rolling pin, on a plate or chopping board) and place it on a sheet of baking parchment, then assemble your toppings. Place the lid of the Dutch oven upside down on to a bed of hot briquettes – the lids that have small integrated feet are best for this. Place your pizza on to the lid, then place the main pan over the top, adding briquettes on top of the base of the pan to create a pizza oven.

- You could also use a **reflector oven** – a flat-pack stainless-steel box that assembles to create a narrow, enclosed back opening into a wide front. The oven is placed next to an open fire with the wider end closest to the flames. Heat from the fire is then reflected by the sides of the oven, creating high temperatures inside it. Pizzas, as well as bread, cookies and anything else you might cook in a conventional oven, can be placed on a cast-iron frying pan and cooked this way, although smaller versions work best due to the limited dimensions. See our recipe for campfire cookies for step-by-step instructions.

- Pizzas can even be made in a **frying pan**, by first shaping the dough and then dropping it into the base of the pan and leaving it for a few minutes to cook and crisp. Turn the pizza over and add toppings to the cooked side. Then cover with a lid or sheet of foil and cook until the cheese is melted.

Dutch oven nachos

COOKED IN A DUTCH OVEN, this big pile of crispy nachos with all the toppings is everything nachos should be, and perfect sharing food with a beer around the fire.

The secret lies in the layering, pairing crunch with soft filling in a thoroughly satisfying way.

SERVES 4

Ingredients

Ready-to-eat good-quality corn nachos – the plainer the better as the toasted corn flavour pairs so well with the toppings.

For the layers:
Tinned beans, drained if necessary – black and refried are our favourites

A jar of tomato-based sauce – a pasta sauce, ready-made salsa or passata is ideal
Grated hard cheese of your choice – a mix works well

For the toppings:
Pickled jalapeño chillies, sliced
Fresh avocado, sliced, or guacamole
Sour cream
Fresh coriander leaves

Equipment

Dutch oven, lined with foil for easy removal and cleaning
Skillet
Charcoal briquettes
Starter chimney
Grater
Knife and chopping board
Large serving plate or bowl

Method

1 Line the Dutch oven with foil – it's a good idea to place the foil on top of a skillet to add protection from the base, otherwise the lowest layer of nachos may burn.
2 Get your briquettes ready in your
3 starter chimney, then use a few to create a base for your oven. Prepare your layer ingredients and toppings.
4 Place a layer of nachos on to the foil in the oven, then add a layer of beans, tomato sauce and grated cheese. You can add chillies as you go, or just use them for topping, depending on how hot you like it! Add another layer of nachos on top.
5 Carry on layering until you've had enough or used up all your ingredients. Finish with a final layer of beans, tomato sauce and cheese.
6 Place the lid on the oven and add a few briquettes on top. Cook for about ten minutes, until the cheese has melted.
7 Carefully lift the nachos out of the oven and place on a serving plate. Top with chillies, avocado/guacamole, sour cream and more cheese, scatter over the fresh coriander leaves, then dive in.

Foraged pesto pasta

PASTA'S A STAPLE in our household, whether we're camping or not. It's perfect for our family's varying tastes, with a few small additions capable of turning a simple child-friendly tomato sauce into something picante and punchy for the grown-ups. This versatility makes it a great choice for camping, along with being good value, easy to store and quick to cook. We've used dried pasta here – penne, fusilli, conchiglie, macaroni and other common shapes all work really well. Spaghetti and linguine are delicious too, but they do demand deft fork skills.

Pesto and other sauces involving finely chopped herbs, and other leafy things, add a lovely freshness to camping cuisine. The greens need to be chopped finely though,

to release all their incredible tastes and aromas. A mezzaluna (a curved, two-handled chopper designed for such things) is good or, if you're going to be doing a lot of this, a hand-operated food processor is brilliant for making houmous, pesto, salsa verde and more on the go. We were given a Zyliss pull-cord version as a gift and, despite our initial skeptisim, it gets a lot of use, plus it's small enough to pack easily and doesn't need electricity.

Foraged pesto is best made in spring, when tender young nettles and wild garlic are abundant. Otherwise, shop-bought leaves including basil and rocket are great, as long as you use them as soon as possible before they start to wilt.

SERVES
4

Ingredients

300g pasta
80g (a large handful)
   of green leaves, such
   as wild garlic, young
   nettles or dandelion
   leaves, rocket or a mix.
   If unavailable, go classic
   with fresh basil
50g nuts – pine nuts are
   the classic addition, but
   cashews, hazelnuts or
   almonds can all work well
50g hard, full-flavoured
   cheese such as
   parmesan or pecorino
1–2 cloves of garlic
150ml olive oil
Water
Salt and pepper to taste

Equipment

Gas burner
Mezzaluna/knife
   and chopping
   board or a
   hand-operated
   blender
Large saucepan
Small pan
Spoon

Method

1 Put the pasta on to cook in a large pan of salty, boiling water.

2 Toast the nuts in a dry pan over a low heat until they're golden. Remove from the pan and leave to cool.

3 Finely chop the leaves, nuts and garlic on a chopping board using a mezzaluna or knife. Scrape into a bowl, add grated cheese and olive oil, mix well and season to taste. If you have a blender, add all the ingredients at once and blend until fairly smooth.

4 When your pasta is cooked (but not over cooked – check regularly as it needs to retain some 'bite'), drain and add the pesto to the pan, stirring it through gently until everything's well covered. Serve with some extra grated cheese and plenty of black pepper.

Family favourite camping curry

WHEN WE LIVED in our bell tent, this filling, tasty curry was a firm favourite all round. We cooked it on our Frontier wood burning stove, with pans balanced on the top, inside the tent over the winter months and out in the field in the summer.

With dishes of fluffy basmati rice, sunshine-yellow dal, and a hearty curry using whatever vegetables we happened to have with us plus tinned chickpeas and a handful of spinach or foraged leaves, it's a colourful celebration of the power of warm food and togetherness and still has a special place in our hearts.

SERVES 4

Ingredients

For the rice:
Basmati rice, enough for 4 plus enough left over for rice pudding (see page 219)

For the dal:
3 cups red lentils
Vegetable stock cube
Thumb-sized piece of fresh root ginger, grated
1–2 garlic cloves, peeled and grated
½ tsp turmeric
½ tsp curry powder
Salt and pepper, to taste

For the curry:
Vegetable oil, for cooking
1–2 onions, peeled and sliced
1 tsp curry powder
1–2 garlic cloves, peeled and grated
Thumb-sized piece of fresh root ginger, grated
400g (14oz) can tinned chopped tomatoes
Mix of prepared vegetables – courgettes, cauliflower, bell peppers, sweetcorn, spinach/foraged greens such as wild garlic or nettles
1 tbsp ground almonds
Salt and pepper, to taste

To serve
Fresh coriander leaves
Yoghurt
Chutneys
Ready-made poppadums

Equipment

Strainer
Two saucepans
Grater
Knife and chopping board
Large saucepan, frying pan or wok
Double-burner stove or two camping stoves

Method

1 Unless you have three available stove tops, make the rice and dal first. These will happily sit to one side and keep their heat while you cook the vegetable curry.

2 To cook the rice, first wash it in plenty of running water then tip it into a saucepan, add twice the volume of water to rice, put the lid on and bring to the boil. Don't stir the rice at any point during cooking. Turn the heat down low and leave it to simmer with the lid on until all the water has been absorbed and the rice is soft and fluffy.

3 To make the dal, first wash the lentils well in running water in a strainer, then tip them into the second saucepan, add twice the volume of water to lentils and put the pan on the heat. Add the stock cube, ginger, garlic, turmeric and curry powder. Stir well and bring to the boil,

stirring regularly. Put a lid on and simmer until the lentils have broken down and the dal is fairly smooth, stirring every so often. Season to taste once cooked.

4 To make the vegetable curry, put the large saucepan, frying pan or wok on the heat and add a good glug of oil. Once the oil is warm, add the sliced onions and cook gently for about ten minutes, until completely softened.

5 Add the curry powder and cook for a minute or so, then add the garlic and ginger and cook for a further minute. If the curry powder starts to stick, add a little water or some of the tinned tomatoes and stir well.

6 Add the vegetables and stir-fry these until softened, adding the tomatoes a little at a time as you go, along with some water if required. Once the vegetables are cooked, add the ground almonds and enough water to make a sauce. Season to taste or add some stock for extra depth of flavour.

7 Serve the rice, dal and vegetable curry on to plates and top with torn coriander leaves. Yoghurt and chutneys make good additions, along with poppadums on the side.

Fast-and-light fish cakes

SATISFYING, AND containing a good amount of high-quality protein, replenishing carbohydrate and salty savouriness, these fish cakes are ideal for backpacking, bikepacking and canoe camping adventures. Mix in one pot and cook in one pan to create a delicious supper on just about any camping stove. If you've been fishing or can get hold of fresh fish, this also works well – just make sure it's thoroughly deboned before using and add an egg (or 1 tbsp dried egg powder) to bind the mixture together. If you're not travelling fast-and-light, this recipe is just as good – perhaps even better – made with real mashed potato.

SERVES
2

Ingredients

Cooking oil, for frying
100g (3½oz) dried potato flakes – go for the 100 per cent potato kind if you can
1 can sustainably sourced fish
A pinch of dried herbs – tarragon or mixed herbs work well
Flour, for dusting/rolling
Salt and pepper, to taste

Equipment

Medium-sized bowl
Spoon
Well-seasoned frying pan
Camping stove or open fire

Method

1   Make up the mashed potato with water, as directed on the packet.
2   Add the fish, herbs and seasoning and mix thoroughly.
3   Shape the mixture into about eight evenly sized balls, roll each one in flour and flatten into a fish cake shape.
4   Heat the oil in a prewarmed frying pan and fry the fish cakes for a few minutes on each side, until golden brown.

Campfire kebabs

FOOD COOKS WELL simply skewered and placed above the embers of a fire, or over hot charcoal briquettes – like a modern barbecue only with a camping twist. Brushing with marinade during cooking adds another dimension to the flavour. Try the Mediterranean vegetable skewers below; add marinated meat, fish, halloumi, tofu or slices of sausage; or for something a little unusual but surprisingly delicious, skewer and cook chestnut or button mushrooms and top with cheese. For a dessert, make tropical fruit skewers with pineapple, banana, mango and coconut brushed with a maple syrup, mint and lime juice marinade.

**SERVES
4**

Ingredients

2–3 bell peppers, deseeded
   and cut into chunks
2 courgettes, trimmed and
   cut into chunks
1 aubergine, cut into slim
   chunks
2 red onions, peeled and cut
   into chunks
Halloumi, cut into thick slices

For the marinade
1 tbsp lemon juice
3 tbsp olive oil
A pinch of dried herbs, or
   snipped or picked rosemary
   or oregano
Salt and pepper, to taste

Equipment

Knife and chopping board
Large bowl
Whisk
Metal skewers, or wooden
   skewers pre-soaked for at
   least half an hour
Glowing embers or hot
   charcoal briquettes

Method

1 Prepare all the vegetables.
2 Whisk together the marinade ingredients in a bowl, then add the vegetables and leave to marinate for about 20 minutes.
3 Thread them on to the skewers, working through the types in order so different vegetables are placed next to each other.
4 Hold the skewers over the glowing embers or place them on the barbecue grill, if using. Brush the vegetables with more marinade as they cook and turn them so all sides are cooked.

SWEET THINGS

Who doesn't love pudding? And even more so if it's
a delicious way to use up leftovers (see rice pudding,
page 219) or utilise the free bounty from the hedgerow
(see crumble, page 216). Fun snacks such as popcorn and
campfire cookies provide entertainment as well as energy.
Children love the excitement of waiting for the first corn
kernels to pop, helping out with mixing the cookie dough
(or just cleaning the bowl afterwards), and gathering the
summer's first crop of juicy blackberries. Warm drinks are
a lovely way to wind down at the end of the day, especially
on those chillier evenings round a campfire under an
open sky, hands wrapped around a steaming mug
of something mulled and delicious.

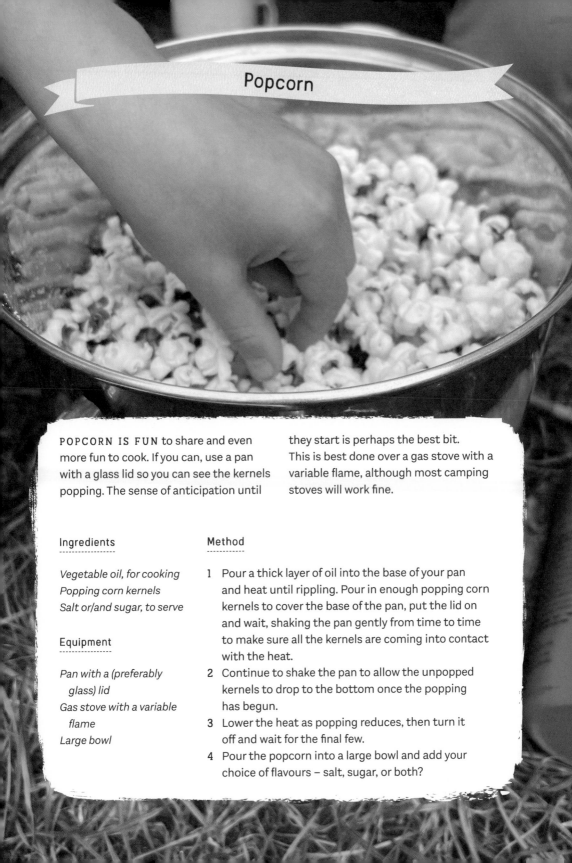

Popcorn

POPCORN IS FUN to share and even more fun to cook. If you can, use a pan with a glass lid so you can see the kernels popping. The sense of anticipation until they start is perhaps the best bit. This is best done over a gas stove with a variable flame, although most camping stoves will work fine.

Ingredients

Vegetable oil, for cooking
Popping corn kernels
Salt or/and sugar, to serve

Equipment

Pan with a (preferably glass) lid
Gas stove with a variable flame
Large bowl

Method

1   Pour a thick layer of oil into the base of your pan and heat until rippling. Pour in enough popping corn kernels to cover the base of the pan, put the lid on and wait, shaking the pan gently from time to time to make sure all the kernels are coming into contact with the heat.
2   Continue to shake the pan to allow the unpopped kernels to drop to the bottom once the popping has begun.
3   Lower the heat as popping reduces, then turn it off and wait for the final few.
4   Pour the popcorn into a large bowl and add your choice of flavours – salt, sugar, or both?

Campfire cookies

THESE ARE A FUN sweet treat to make with children, and just as popular with grown-ups. They work well in a Dutch oven and cook quickly so they're a good thing to pop in after you've baked bread or similar. Otherwise, set up a reflector oven next to an open fire and cook them in that.

MAKES
12

Ingredients

75g (2½oz) butter, plus a little extra for greasing
75g (2½oz) sugar
50g (1¾oz) cocoa powder
125g (4½oz) self-raising flour
1 egg or equivalent powdered egg made up as per packet instructions
A scattering of chocolate chips

Equipment

Reflector oven or Dutch oven plus an open fire
Small baking tray or cast-iron pan that fits in the reflector oven, if using
Measuring cup or weighing scales
Small saucepan
Wooden spoon
Spatula

Method

1 Preheat the oven – if using a Dutch oven, use the table on page 180 to achieve a temperature of about 180°C (350°F). Grease the baking tray or pan.
2 Melt the butter and sugar over a low heat in the saucepan. Allow to cool a little and then add the cocoa powder and flour, stirring well to mix. Add the egg, continuing to mix until fully combined.
3 Spoon the mixture out into 12 balls of an equal size and place them on the greased baking tray or pan, flattening each slightly and leaving space between for spreading. You may need to bake these in several batches.
4 Bake in the reflector oven or Dutch oven for about ten minutes or until cooked but still a little squidgy in the centre.
5 Transfer each cookie carefully on to a plate using the spatula.

Hedgerow crumble

STEWING FRUIT is a great way to use up that bag of apples you brought along on your camping trip that no one now wants because they're bruised. If you're camping in late summer or early autumn and are lucky enough to be pitched near to an orchard, woodland or fruitful hedgerow, it's also a wonderful way to celebrate the abundance of this time of year. Apples, plums (and their smaller relatives, including Mirabelle plums, damsons and greengages) and berries, such as wild blackberries, raspberries and bilberries, are all perfect for adding to the mix. Just be careful you're 100 per cent certain about your ID skills to avoid the wrong berries going in.

Fruit can be simply cooked down in a lidded pan until soft and served with yoghurt, custard or, if there's a campsite shop that sells it, vanilla ice cream. Sprinkle granola or a toasted mix of oats, nuts, dried fruit and maple syrup over the top for an easy, instant crumble. A more traditional crumble works superbly in a Dutch oven.

**SERVES
4**

Ingredients

Fruit – a single type of fruit,
   such as apples, or a mixture
   of apples, pears, plums and
   berries
1 cup plain flour
1 cup oats
Sugar, to taste
About 50g butter, cubed,
   or 50ml olive oil
A handful of nuts and seeds
   or ground almonds
Tinned custard, to serve

Equipment

Reflector oven or Dutch oven
   plus an open fire
Chimney starter
Knife and chopping board
Measuring cup
Mixing bowl

Method

1   Prepare your cooking area by heating briquettes in a chimney starter and laying a few as a base for your Dutch oven.
2   Wash and prepare the fruit, slicing any harder fruit such as apples and pears so they cook more quickly. Arrange a good layer of the fruit in the base of the Dutch oven.
3   Make the crumble topping by mixing together the flour and oats with sugar to taste and enough butter or olive oil to form a crumbly mixture. Add some nuts and seeds for extra texture and goodness if you like. Ground almonds also work well.
4   Tip the crumble layer on top of the fruit, pat it down, then put on the lid, place the oven on the briquettes and add more briquettes to the top.
5   Cook for 20–30 minutes, until the crumble is browned and the fruit bubbling. Serve with warm custard.

Leftover rice pudding

ON A DRIZZLY AFTERNOON in the tent, we'll admit to having eaten cold tinned rice pudding straight from the can with a spoon. However, the piping hot, home-made version, though it takes a little time and attention, is infinitely better. Even better still, it's a great way to use up leftover rice, which is otherwise hard to store safely while camping. We've suggested serving your rice pudding in the traditional way – with a spoonful of jam! But feel free to be more creative with toppings – a good grating of nutmeg or chocolate, some sliced banana or pear, or a handful of berries all go well.

NB. The exact quantity of milk required depends on how much rice is left over but using approximately the same volume of milk as cooked rice gives you about the right consistency. You can always add a little more milk if needed.

Ingredients

Cooked rice
Milk (dairy or otherwise – aim for about the same as the volume of rice)
Sugar or maple syrup, to taste
Vanilla extract (optional)
Jam to serve

Equipment

Pan
Stove
Measuring cup
Wooden spoon

Method

1 Put the cooked rice, milk, sugar or maple syrup, and some vanilla extract if you have it, into a large pan.
2 Cook over a medium heat, stirring continuously, until thick and creamy.
3 Ladle into bowls and serve with a good spoonful of jam.

Baked banana splits

BANANAS COOK BRILLIANTLY in their skins on a barbecue, in the glowing embers of a fire or in a pizza oven or Dutch oven after the main course, becoming something even more delicious, especially when combined with some fun toppings.

Ingredients

Bananas

Toppings, such as maple syrup, chocolate buttons, marshmallows, Nutella or even ice cream if there's a campsite shop nearby!

Equipment

Knife

Barbecue, glowing embers of a fire (wrap the bananas in aluminium foil to protect them if cooking this way), pizza oven or Dutch oven

Method

1 Cook the bananas whole until the skins have blackened all over, then split the skins along the concave length.
2 Either scoop out the hot, soft banana into a bowl or eat it straight from the skin, topping with your choice of treats.

Mulled cider/apple juice

THERE'S SOMETHING ABOUT the particular mix of spices in a good mulling blend that's warming on a deeper level. Perhaps it's the connection with Christmases past, or the hint of warmer climes still captured in the dried spice.

Whatever it is, heating and mulling cider, apple juice or even wine, if you can break free from the Christmas connotations – unless of course you're camping at Christmas – makes it extra cosy, and a perfect camping beverage.

Ingredients

Cider or apple juice
Cinnamon sticks
1 orange
Cloves
Sugar, to taste

Equipment

Large saucepan
Stove

Method

1 Pour the cider or apple juice into a large pan. Add a couple of sticks of cinnamon and an orange stuck all over with cloves.
2 Heat gently – the longer you can leave it to infuse, the stronger the spicing will be. Sweeten if desired before serving in mugs.

Campfire hot chocolate

THERE CAN'T BE much more satisfying
than sitting around the fire pit after a long
day's adventuring hugging a mug of proper
hot chocolate. Don't be tempted by the
insipid imitations of real hot chocolate
that come in packets and to which you just
add water. These will only make you feel
cheated. Instead, take along a packet of
good-quality chocolate flakes or the solid
version, which you can grate as required.
Grated drinking chocolate is also fantastic
over porridge or baked bananas.

Ingredients

Milk
Chocolate flakes
  or solid drinking
  chocolate, grated

Equipment

Large saucepan
Stove
Grater
Wooden spoon

Method

Warm the milk (but don't let it boil) in the
saucepan, then simply stir in the chocolate
flakes or grate in the drinking chocolate and
mix until well combined. Serve in mugs.

05

Adventure
time!

Camping is an adventure in its own right. From planning, sorting out kit, packing and travelling to setting up camp and living under canvas, it's an experience completely unlike staying in a hotel or holiday cottage. But camping can also be an integral part of a bigger adventure, allowing you to head out into wild and uninhabited places, providing you with shelter and privacy wherever you choose to take it.

Most people think of car camping and backpacking as the two obvious choices for camping trips. However, the list of potential adventures is much longer and more varied. Minimalist, lightweight kit combined with bags designed specifically for the demands of adventures on two wheels or wild water mean camping is possible even when space is very limited. This section explores some of the ways in which camping can be an integral part of bigger adventures such as bikepacking, kayak camping and packrafting, and what you'll need to get started.

The list of potential adventures is much longer and more varied when on two wheels or over wild water … camping is possible even when space is very limited

▶ Bikepacking adventure in the Bannau Brycheinog (Brecon Beacons) National Park. All camping, cooking and spare kit for a couple of nights packed in lightweight bike bags

Car camping

Most people start out car camping, and it's a great way to get accustomed to the different pace of life. Whether you're camping as a couple, with friends or as a family holiday, it's a brilliantly affordable means of getting away. People feel nostalgic about camping holidays because of fond childhood memories, and it's an opportunity to create new memories to feel nostalgic about in the future, too. Packing is always a big part of car camping trips, though space is at far less of a premium than it is when you need to carry all your kit, so there's definitely room for a few more luxuries. Despite that extra room, however, it's amazing how often we find our car crammed to the rafters with all the things we had no idea we needed to take.

While having the right kit for a camping trip is important, it's easy to get carried away by the vast range of gadgets and gear available in camping shops. Try to remember that a big part of the joy of camping lies in its simplicity and there's a delicate balance to be found between convenience and detracting from the experience. It is perfectly possible to basically recreate your home kitchen in temporary form inside your tent, but do you really need – or want – to?

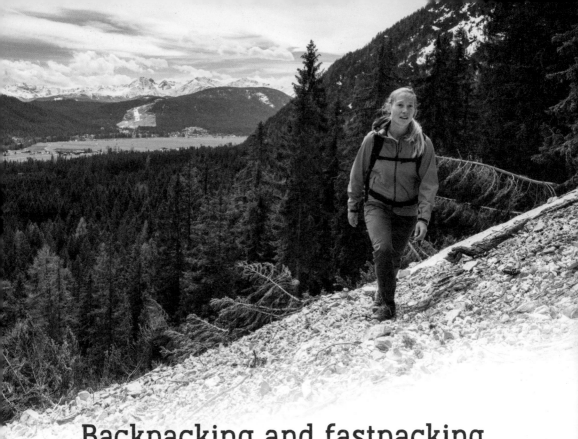

Backpacking and fastpacking

Backpacking, and its fast-and-light relative, fastpacking, is the ultimate in self-sufficient adventuring. Whether you're carrying everything you need for a mid-week night on a hill, a weekend away or a lengthy excursion on a long-distance trail, backpacking is a way of travelling and living that's customisable to suit the size of adventure you want and how much time you have available to do it.

In general, a lighter-weight set-up will mean that the walking is more enjoyable, and you'll be more able to comfortably cover greater distances each day. But a minimalist approach will necessarily mean sacrificing some warmth and comfort in return for a reduction in weight. One of the many joys of this type of camping is the puzzle involved in finding the perfect balance between a light pack and a comfortable night's sleep.

How to pack and adjust a rucksack for backpacking

Even if you're planning to go as lightweight as possible, backpacking trips that involve an overnight camp require quite a lot of kit. So, choosing the best pack for you and your kit, adjusting it properly, and packing it well will ensure your trip is as enjoyable as possible. A systematic approach to packing also helps reduce the likelihood of forgetting anything important...

To fit a rucksack, follow these steps:

1 Start with all the straps loose.

2 Adjust the back length of the rucksack to match your back. Different packs have different ways of doing this, but most will have a system that slides the shoulder strap attachment point up or down to match your back length. Adjust it to what you expect and then fine-tune to fit. The perfect fit is when the waist strap is around the hip bones and the shoulder straps follow the shape of your shoulder.

3 Tighten the waist belt so that the padded strap is around and slightly above your hip bones. The waist belt should take about 80 per cent of the weight of the pack.

4 Tighten the main shoulder straps until they are snug. Overtightening these will lift the weight off the hip belt and on to your shoulders.

5 Tighten the load lifter straps. Tightening these straps makes the pack more stable but takes some of the weight off the waist belt. Make them taut but not tight for normal walking and tighter for more stability on technical ground.

6 Do up the chest strap so that it's flat but not restrictive.

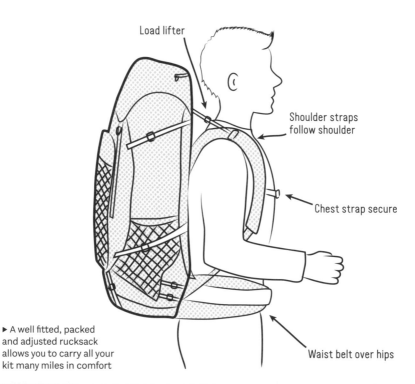

Load lifter

Shoulder straps follow shoulder

Chest strap secure

Waist belt over hips

▶ A well fitted, packed and adjusted rucksack allows you to carry all your kit many miles in comfort

Where you're going, including the underfoot terrain and availability of shops and campsites, how long you're going for and the likely weather conditions will all combine to determine exactly what and how much kit you need; this then dictates the size of your pack. Most people will take the smallest pack they can comfortably get all the kit into – there's no point in carrying extra weight or bulk. Your sleeping system, clothing, cooking gear and emergency kit won't change very much whether you're heading out for a single night's micro-adventure or a multi-day backpacking trip, but the amount of food and fuel you need can vary dramatically. Extra food and fuel space is therefore the main reason for larger bags on expeditions and longer trips. If there will be shops and resupply is easy, then a smaller, lighter bag may suffice even on a long trip.

Here are our suggested pack volumes:

- One night to a few days' lightweight backpacking or running: 15–30 litres
- One night to one week backpacking: 40–70 litres
- Expedition or longer trips when resupply is infrequent: 70–110 litres

If you need to buy a new pack for a trip, the two key things are the volume and the fit. If you're not sure about the volume it's perfectly acceptable to bring a few key bulky items (tent, sleeping bag, mat, jacket) to the shop so you can test-pack potential bags and work out the size you need. Good outdoor shops will allow you to put a couple of climbing ropes or some weighted bags into rucksacks before trying them to get a better idea of how they feel with weight in. An empty bag is normally comfortable, but a heavy bag must fit you to be comfortable.

Many packs will come in several back length sizes to give you the best and most comfortable fit. Packs also come in either a men's or women's version or a unisex and slim fit, depending on the make. Men tend to have longer backs, wider shoulders and narrower hips than women so it makes sense to have different fits. Shorter, slighter males may find a slim/female fit works better and taller, broader women may find the unisex/male fit works better. Most larger rucksacks will also have an adjustable back length so that you can fine-

How to pack a rucksack

KEY

Light items with easy access

Heaviest items

Lightest items

Midweight items

tune the fit. You will need to adjust this to your back length before you test the pack. Shop staff should be able to help and advise how best to fit each design of pack but it's useful to know how this works and what you are aiming for.

The rucksack is designed to carry weight stably and efficiently by loading your hips rather than your shoulders. To help it work as well as possible, you need to pack the bag with the heaviest items close to your back, above the waist belt and lower than your neck. This keeps the centre of gravity close to your own centre of gravity and helps the bag feel stable. If you pack heavy items further away from your body, the bag will feel like it swings, heavy items in the base pull you backwards, and heavy items at the top feel unstable. Most hikers advise imagining your pack has four separate packing zones to pack most effectively.

1 The base is for mid-weight items, such as your sleeping bag, mat and clothes.
2 The heaviest items, such as a hydration system, stove, tent, food and fuel, go against your back.
3 The lightest items, such as clothing and a towel, pack in front of the heavy items to keep them in place.
4 Lightweight and quick-access items go at the top and in the lid. This is where your waterproofs, first aid kit, torch and some snacky food go.

Packing following this system will make it easiest and most comfortable to carry the load. It's worth following this advice even with small and light fastpacking set-ups, to keep the bag as balanced as possible. Very few rucksacks are fully waterproof, so we always use a lightweight drybag to line the main pack, at the very least packing important items such as our sleeping bags and spare clothes in small drybags.

To make packing easy and avoid forgetting anything, follow these steps:

1. Lay everything out before you pack it.
2. Open the bag and loosen all the compression straps.
3. If you are using a hydration reservoir, fill this and pack it first: it's very hard to get it in if you've already packed the bag. Don't pack the hydration bladder inside your drybag; if it leaks, the drybag should keep the rest of your kit dry.
4. Pack your sleeping bag at the bottom of the pack and fill in any extra space in the base with the sleeping mat and clothes.
5. Arrange the heaviest items you're carrying as close to your back as you can fit them. Add lightweight clothing and other kit to keep them in place.
6. Add your waterproofs, snacks and all the other small items that you might need regularly or quickly to the lid and hip pockets.
7. Fill and add water or fuel bottles to the side pockets.
8. Strap on any tent poles, trekking poles or other kit to the accessory straps.
9. Tighten all compression straps to stabilise the load.

Once it's filled with kit, a large rucksack can be a pretty heavy, unwieldy thing and surprisingly tricky to put on. Here's how to go about it as safely and smoothly as possible:

1. Stand the pack on the ground and make sure the straps are loosened.
2. Go down on one knee facing the pack and using the top haul loop, lift it on to your knee with the straps facing you.
3. Twist so that you can get one arm through the strap and on to your shoulder while still supporting the bag with your knee.
4. Lean forwards and stand, getting your other arm through the other strap as you do.
5. Do up the waist belt first to get the weight off your shoulders.
6. Do up and tighten the other straps.

What to take backpacking and fastpacking

A well-fitting rucksack, large enough to carry all your essentials but small enough to be able to carry comfortably over long distances and, depending on where you're heading, rough terrain, is the first consideration. If you can, head to a good outdoor shop with your kit and try on a few different rucksacks while they're packed with your kit – then you can get the balance exactly right.

Supportive footwear is essential when you're carrying a heavy pack as your feet will experience forces that are both larger and differently distributed than normal. When we're carrying a heavy rucksack, we move our centre of mass further forwards to counterbalance the weight on our back.

This increases the forces through our feet and moves them further forwards, adding extra load to the arch and front of the foot. A sturdy pair of walking boots that offer grip and protection underfoot, support for the arch and cushioning for the front of the foot, as well as adjustable support throughout the foot and ankle are usually the best option. Many walking boots are also waterproof, keeping your feet dry and reducing the risk of blisters. Always pair them up with a good pair of socks – Merino wool socks, often with some nylon for added durability, offer a great combination of comfort, cushioning and natural microbe, moisture and temperature regulation.

Fastpacking is growing in popularity, combining the freedom and self-sufficiency of backpacking with trail running's ability to cover longer distances in less time. Far more so than walking, comfortable running requires a minimalist approach to packing, including a running-specific pack, which will stay firmly in place even when you're moving at speed over rough ground. There's little room for luxuries as every gram makes a difference to your ability to run. Elite competitors at mountain marathons – usually involving two full days running around in remote places with an overnight camp, carrying everything for the duration in a pack including tent, sleeping bag, mat, food, stove and spare clothing – have been known to take bubble wrap to sleep on as it's so much lighter than a camping mat. Whether you go to those extremes or you're willing to carry a little extra weight and bulk in return for a good night's sleep is a decision only you can make.

Where to go

Backpacking with a tent opens up a vast variety of opportunities for adventures. Long-distance trails stretch around the world, with each country and region having its own network, traditions and support systems. Explore the National Trails in England and Wales, Scotland's Great Trails, the Grande Randonnée (GR) routes across Europe, America's Triple Crown (the Appalachian Trail, Pacific Crest Trail and Continental Divide Trail), New Zealand's Te Araroa – which means 'Long Pathway' in the native Māori language, the Camino de Santiago ('Way of St James') and many, many more, spanning hundreds of thousands of miles.

For those who prefer to watch the countryside pass by more quickly but cover far greater distances, inter-railing is experiencing a resurgence in popularity, offering an easy and relaxed means of travelling between cities, National Parks or long-distance trails.

▼ Lightweight tents at the overnight camp during the OMM (Original Mountain Marathon) in the UK

Bikepacking and cycle touring

Born from the long-distance self-supported bike races in the USA, bikepacking takes the much-loved sport of cycle touring, where bulky panniers and racks are supported by a sturdy touring bike, and updates it, allowing you to take your adventures off-road and into the wilds with a lightweight, streamlined set-up. Cleverly designed bikepacking bags allow you to distribute your kit around your bike, meaning the riding is more enjoyable, the bike handling is improved, and everything's positioned just where you need it.

The ingenious design of bikepacking kit also means a much wider range of bikes to choose from than is possible with the traditional cycle touring set-up based around bulky racks and panniers.

It's likely, therefore, that a bike you already own will do the job brilliantly. But if you're looking for a new steed, your choice depends on the terrain you'll be taking on and your preference for handling, position and general riding. As you're likely to be spending many hours a day in the saddle, a bike that fits perfectly is essential. Bikepacking bags work well on road, gravel and mountain bikes; some brands even make bikes designed specifically for bikepacking. In general, a bike with a standard triangle frame works best as it allows you to attach a frame bag for maximum carrying capacity.

▲ A typical three pack bikepacking set up using a combination of Ortlieb and Vaude bags on a hardtail mountain bike

[237]

JEN: 'In my early 20s, struggling to work out what I wanted to do with life, I decided to go on an adventure. I needed a bike anyway, as I didn't drive, but other than that the trip had to be as cheap as possible, so I planned to cycle around Ireland. Spending 12 hours a day working in a call centre, often with evening shifts at a pub, I eventually saved up enough to buy myself a bike, cycle touring bags (these were the days before the invention of superlight bikepacking kit), a tent, sleeping bag, stove and everything else I thought I might need and could fit on to the bike. By the time I was ready to go, the whole set-up was so top heavy I could barely keep it upright when stationary. But Ireland was incredible, and the experience shaped me, building my self-confidence, showing me wild places and wild things, and igniting a passion for self-sufficient adventures and the simple joy of living under canvas. I spent three months on the road, cycling during the day and sleeping in my tiny tent at night, inching my way around the beautiful Irish coastline and visiting the mountains, towns, villages and countryside within reach along the way. I'd cycle up to 60 miles (97km) each day, up and down steep hills, through relentless rain, grateful for the waterproofness of my tent and the kindness of Irish strangers who often took pity on me and with whom I spent many an enjoyable evening sharing Guinness and folk music. Looking back, it's the kind of immersive experience only made possible through the connectedness with places and people that comes with walking, cycling and camping – almost a vulnerability, which can feel a little daunting at the time but is enormously rewarding retrospectively.'

What to take

Once you've decided on the bike you'll be using for your bikepacking adventures, the next step is to kit it out with bags for carrying everything you'll need to stay warm, dry and well fed along the way. When choosing kit for bikepacking, weight and size are the primary considerations as you'll be carrying everything you need, so the lighter your set-up, the more enjoyable your ride will be. On the flip side, packing super-light may mean you're colder and less comfortable at night, so it's important to get the balance right.

▶ Bikepacking with gravel bikes

How to pack for bikepacking

MOST BIKEPACKING set-ups include a frame bag, seat pack, handlebar roll and up to four small accessory bags. Water is generally carried in bottle cages, which sit low down and within the frame. You can also carry a small rucksack or waist pack if needed, but it's more comfortable to carry the weight on the bike if you can.

The specifics of the trip, including the weather and terrain, the length of the trip, the geometry and size of the bike and personal preference will all determine the finer details of your bike and bag set-up, but there are a few general rules that most riders follow:

● Carry the heaviest items low and central to keep the bike as stable as possible.
● Keep the handlebar bag light to minimise the effects on steering and handling.
● Use an easy-to-reach top tube or stem bag to store regularly used items and snacks.
● Use tent poles or rolled clothing to provide structure for your seat bag and handlebar bag.
● If you choose to carry a rucksack, keep it as light as possible. If you're carrying a hydration bladder, drink this before your bike-mounted water bottles, which are better positioned for efficient carrying.
● Use drybags to keep important things, such as your sleeping bag and spare clothes, dry.

Bikepacking: what to pack and where to pack it

● **Frame bag:** Heavy items such as spare parts, tools, stove, fuel and food.

● **Seat pack:** Spare clothing and extra food – place the heaviest items closest to the bike.

● **Handlebar roll/pack:** Tent/bivi bag/tarp plus sleeping bag and mat. Tent poles can be strapped on top of the bag separately or along the top tube if they don't fit in the bag.

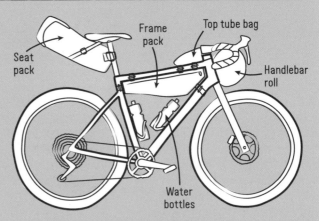

● **Accessory bags:** Snacks, phone, camera, wallet, map, compass, torch.

● **Bottle cages:** Water.

Cycle touring: what to pack and where to pack it

● **Front panniers:** Tools, spare parts, stove, cooking equipment, food and fuel.

● **Rear panniers:** Sleeping system (sleeping bag, mat and tent/bivi) and clothing. Extra food if necessary.

● **Saddle bag:** A small bag to keep out of the way of rear rack-mounted items. Easy to access, it should contain a spare inner tube, puncture repair kit and multi-tool.

● **Handlebar bag:** Snacks and regular-use items such as phone, map, torch and camera.

● **Frame-mounted bottle holders:** Water and bike pump.

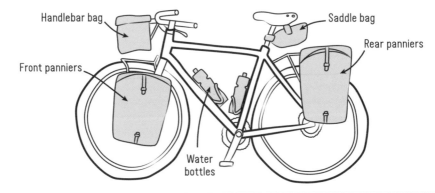

How to pack for cycle touring

Classic cycle touring bikes have panniers on the front forks and at the back. They also use a handlebar-mounted bag, a small saddle bag and make use of the multiple bottle cage mounts on the main frame. This set-up allows you to carry more volume and weight than a bikepacking set-up but it's heavier, affects the bike's handling more and is less aerodynamic.

When packing a cycle touring set-up, about 60 per cent of the overall weight should be in the front panniers with lighter, bulkier items in the rear panniers. A tent can be strapped on top of the rear panniers if you need to save pannier space. Try to keep the handlebar bag light, as too much weight here can make the steering very tricky indeed, especially in windy conditions. This set-up should make the bike balanced and nicest to ride. Most panniers are waterproof, but we think it's well worth using lightweight drybags in your panniers just in case. It's especially important to

▼ Touring cycling with Ortlieb panniers

keep your sleeping bag and spare clothes dry and drybags don't weigh much.

Where to go

A bikepacking adventure can take place over a single day, a weekend, a week or much longer. With far fewer limitations on the type of terrain than in traditional touring, the route is yours to imagine.

Although a good bikepacking set-up opens up a wide range of trails and terrains for riding, you'll still need to take care how and where you go. Check the laws for cycling off-road specific to the country you're visiting, along with those for camping if you're hoping to wild camp (see our section on wild camping in Chapter 2). In England and Wales, for example, off-road cycling is permitted on:

- bridleways – always give way to pedestrians and horse riders
- Byways Open to All Traffic (BOAT) – also used by off-road motor vehicles so take extra care

- restricted byways – open to pedestrians, cyclists, horse riders and non-mechanically propelled vehicles
- green lanes where permission exists
- permissive paths – at the landowner's concession

Cycling is not permitted on footpaths or most open access land such as moorland. In Scotland, there's much greater access for bikes; however, all cyclists must adhere to the Scottish Outdoor Access Code:

- Take responsibility for your own actions.
- Respect the interests of other people.
- Care for the environment.

In the USA, bikepacking is generally permitted on public lands. The website bikepacking.com is an excellent and comprehensive source of information, based in the USA but with inspiration for routes across the world.

Kayak and canoe camping

Camping by boat opens up the opportunity to explore lakes, rivers and coastal areas, paddling out to camp on hidden beaches and remote islands inaccessible any other way. Because a canoe or kayak has to float, however, kit choice and how you pack it is important. Particularly with a sea kayak, while weight isn't a huge issue as long as everything's packed correctly, the size and shape of the

TOP TIP

PADDLING SAFETY

If you're considering heading out in a kayak or canoe, boat handling and water safety skills, as well as knowing where you can and cannot paddle, are essential. There are many excellent adventure providers with experienced and knowledgeable guides who can take you out on single- or multi-day trips safely and responsibly. Canoe and kayak clubs are another great way to learn the skills required for bigger adventures and meet and learn from like-minded people. We'd highly recommend starting out this way if you're not already an experienced paddler.

▶ Sea kayak adventure in Arisaig on the west coast of Scotland

kit you take is dictated by the dimensions of the compartments into which is has to fit.

Kayak or canoe?

Kayaks are fully covered boats designed for one or two people to sit in. Sit-on-top models are available, and these are great for day trips and beginner paddlers as they're easy to fall out of should they capsize, but they're not well designed for transporting camping gear. Canoes are open boats, meaning you can fit far more kit inside them than you can in a kayak and the size and shape of your cargo is less important. However, waterproofing everything is more difficult and canoes also tend to be less manoeuvrable than kayaks, both on the water and should you need to carry (portage) your boat, so they may not be suitable for all adventures.

Kayaks are designed to hold a lot of weight and still move efficiently, but an unbalanced boat will be hard to handle, which could be dangerous. Try out packing before you go, checking your trim in calm, shallow water and adjusting the load until the balance is right. Place any kit that's not waterproof in drybags before stowing them in the boat, securing the storage hatches before setting out. If you're paddling a sit-on-top, make sure everything is in waterproof bags and firmly secured to the boat before you leave.

What to take

Some longer or larger items like tent poles can be tricky to fit into a kayak, particularly those using sit-in style boats with small hatch openings. In this case, a tarp or hammock may be a good option for shelter, particularly if the weather is looking calm.

With space at a premium, the more items you can take that have more than one

▲ An idyllic kayak camping set up with a freestanding Hilleberg tent and Trangia stove

use, the better. Paddles double brilliantly as tent poles, lifejackets as pillows, and the boat itself as a wall to your shelter or an anchor for guy lines. Our pitching guide in Chapter 1 has some useful guidance on pitching on sandy and stony ground. When camping on beaches or other tidal areas, always be aware of the tides, pitching your tent and storing your boat well clear of the incoming water.

Unless you're freshwater paddling and have a decent water filter, you'll need to carry water with you. Kayaks can hold plenty of water – enough for several days' paddling – but because it's heavy you'll need to pack water stores centrally, close to where you sit, or use it as ballast to balance your boat.

All kit should be packed into small (3–5-litre) drybags before it's stowed in your kayak hatches. If you have a bigger kayak, you might get away with bigger bags, but it's still a good idea to use several in case you get a hole or leak in one.

You'll find a comprehensive set of kit lists for camping on foot, wheels or water at the end of this book.

How to pack a sea kayak

Sea kayaks are stable and efficient to paddle, enabling travel over long distances and across open water to reach remote camping spots. The closed deck makes them more weatherproof than a canoe, but it also limits the volume you can carry. The size of the storage access ports limits the size of any individual item you take. Manufacturers will give each model a maximum load capacity. To find out how much camping kit you can safely carry, add your weight to the weight of the paddle, your kayak clothing, buoyancy aid, helmet and emergency kit and take this away from the maximum quoted weight to give the maximum kit weight.

Sea kayaks usually have a front and a rear storage compartment. Some also have an easily reachable day storage area, located just behind the cockpit. You need to balance the kayak by packing about the same weight in the front and the rear compartments. A top tip is to pack all the kit into two large carry bags and balance them out, then pack the kit from one bag into the back and the other bag into the front. Pack everything in small drybags to keep the gear organised and provide additional water protection. It's good practice to pack all the electrical and metal kit in the rear compartment so that it's further away and less likely to interfere with the compass. Pack the large carry bags in last on top of everything else so that they come out first and make it easy to carry your kit from the kayak to camp. Pack snacks, navigation, communication and emergency kit within reach of the cockpit so that you can access them while paddling.

Once packed and before setting off,

check the trim of the kayak: the stern should sit very slightly lower than the bow. Adjust your packing if necessary to trim the kayak correctly.

How to pack a canoe

Open canoes are great for camping adventures as they can carry a substantial amount of weight and volume and they are easy to pack. A canoe will have a manufacturer's recommended weight capacity, so when you're working out what to take, make sure you and your personal kit (paddles, buoyancy aid etc), plus all the essential kit for your trip, weigh in under that amount. Then you can decide whether or not you pack that extra pair of shoes.

All your kit needs to be well secured and waterproof using drybags and storage

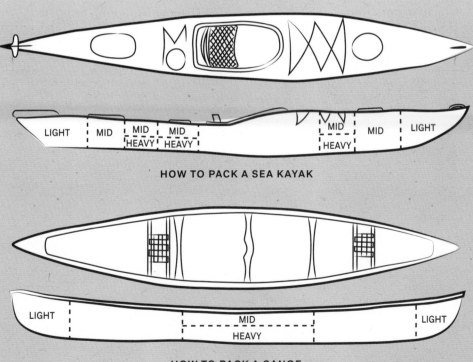

HOW TO PACK A SEA KAYAK

HOW TO PACK A CANOE

barrels. Unlike a covered kayak, everything in your canoe will be open to the elements. Tough waterproof bags and buoyant canoe barrels are available for this exact purpose.

Think about how you will carry the kit to and from the canoe and during any portages, and between the high water line and your overnight camp. Large waterproof bags with carry handles such as bags for life or similar work well.

Pack the heaviest items lowest and most centrally within the canoe for the best handling and balance. Try to avoid packing anything higher than the gunwales – this keeps the canoe balanced and doesn't increase the surface area the wind has to catch and blow your boat around. It's best to do a test pack in the garden if possible before you set off to make sure everything fits, and you have enough straps to secure everything. When you start out, you may need to adjust the load slightly to balance the canoe; this can often be done simply by moving heavy drinking water or fuel forwards or backwards in the canoe.

A note on inflatable canoes and kayaks

Inflatable canoes and kayaks can be a good option for day trips as they're packable and relatively cheap. However, they're not usually light or packable enough to be carried far and may fall prey to punctures, which could be disastrous should you be caught far from land. They're often far less easy to control than fixed boats, so may not be suitable for longer adventures.

Where to go

Exploring by boat opens up the possibility for camping trips on lakes, lochs, rivers, canals and coastal areas. Depending on where you go, you may be free to paddle and camp where you please (as long as you do so responsibly, of course) or you may need to buy a licence to paddle and a camping pitch for the overnight stays. Rules and regulations vary widely so remember to check the specific requirements for where you're going before you go.

In the UK, access to rivers is often difficult and contested as a result of private ownership. However, some rivers have long-established canoe/kayaking traditions, with campsites dotted along their banks ready and waiting for tired paddlers.

If you're paddling on rivers or canals you will often need permission. In the UK, a navigation licence can be purchased from the Canal & River Trust, or from the local navigations office. Membership of British Canoeing includes a licence and supports the organisation's important work improving access rights for paddlers. There are some exceptions where a licence is not required, including for 100 beautiful miles (160km) of the River Wye – from Hay-on-Wye downstream to the river's confluence with the Severn Estuary at Chepstow – a stretch that has benefited from a public right of navigation since the 17th century. Further afield, here are some suggested canoe/kayak camping adventures:

Norway

With its vast number of fjords and permissive attitude to wild camping, Norway offers almost endless scope for water-based camping. Try Sognefjorden – also known as the 'King of the Fjords'

Plan your own adventure if you're an experienced paddler or hire a guide or join a group to be guided by a local, knowledgeable expert.

– which is Norway's largest and deepest fjord. Stretching for 127 miles (204km) inland from the coast north of Bergen, and reaching depths of 1,300m (4,265ft) in places, this UNESCO-designated fjord is dotted with settlements, forest-cloaked hillsides, dramatic rocky peaks and numerous inlets to explore.

Scotland

Scotland benefits from more relaxed wild camping rules than the rest of the UK, and its intricate coastline is perfect for exploring by kayak. On the west coast, Arisaig is dotted with tiny, uninhabited islands (unless you count the resident otters) and white sandy beaches. Plan your own adventure if you're an experienced paddler or hire a guide or join a group to benefit from and be guided by a local, knowledgeable expert.

Sweden

With more islands than any other country on earth, Sweden is a sea kayaker's paradise. Wild camping is widely permitted, leaving you free to paddle between the islands and pitch up where you choose. Try the Saint Anna archipelago, which lies on Sweden's east coast, south of Stockholm. This archipelago boasts 6,000 islets and islands, many of which are uninhabited.

Packrafting and bikerafting

Packrafting evolved in the USA, starting out with inflatable boats left over from WWII being sold in military surplus stores and used by enterprising adventurers to explore previously inaccessible waters. In the 1950s, these early packrafts were used to descend Mexico's Copper Canyon and Tasmania's Franklin River. From these foundations, packrafts evolved, firstly with designs best suited to flat water, and then those capable of running rivers and handling whitewater.

In the 2000s, adventurer Thor Tingey and his mother, Sheri, who was both an experienced kayaker and a dab hand with a sewing machine, started exploring ways to improve the old Sevylor inflatable kayaks to make them suitable for wilderness exploration. After years of experimentation and improvement, they launched their own company, Alpacka Raft, which now produces a range of top-quality packrafts to suit every adventure. Blending the lightweight packability – equivalent in size and weight to a two-person backpacking tent – that allows rafts to be carried many miles by bike or backpack, with durability, safety and superior handling, packrafting has opened up a whole new world of adventure possibility. In the words of current co-owner Sarah Tingey: 'Packrafts inspire adventurers to reimagine backcountry travel. In reimagining it, every person has the possibility of experiencing the freedom,

▼ Alpacka Raft in Kodiak, Alaska (*below*) and Westwater, Utah (*right*)

solitude, and joy of accessing remote landscapes.'

If you're considering dipping your toe in the watery world of packrafting, be aware it's a deep one. From the initial outlay (packrafts don't come cheap) to the time investment required in order to learn how to pilot one effectively and safely, it's a sizeable undertaking. But for those who have a regular opportunity to visit remote and beautiful stretches of water inaccessible other than on foot, it's a labour of love that's heartily repaid by the rewards.

What to take

Aside from your packraft and buoyancy aid and a folding paddle – ideally one that folds into four for easy packing – you'll need a light, strong rucksack with enough storage space for these items and everything else you'll require for the duration of your trip. If you're bikepacking/bikerafting, the rucksack only needs to contain your raft, paddle and associated kit (inflation bag, waterproofs) as the rest can go in your bike bags as normal. By its nature, packrafting opens up access to some remote and difficult-to-access places, but this means that shops and pubs are likely to be few and far between – or even nonexistent – so self-sufficiency is important.

The essence of packrafting is in the quick and relatively easy transitions it allows between hiking/biking and paddling. You'll therefore need to be able to carry your packraft in your backpacking or bikepacking storage and then lash your pack (and bike if biking) to the raft for paddling. For the same reason, it's also well worth doing plenty of inflating/deflating practice before you head out into the wilds to make these transitions

◄ The Grand Canyon on an Alpacka Raft

bike and kit. For the more experienced, linking up groups of islands or coastal headlands, or descending rivers all provide varying levels of challenge, each with its own specific set of logistical and practical considerations.

as smooth as possible. Should you reach any sections you're not happy to paddle, your packraft needs to be carried or rapidly deflated in order to portage it to the next section of paddle-able water.

Where to go

As with other water-based camping adventures, your best bet if you're starting out packrafting is to hire an expert guide or book on to a course. Learning from someone who has a wealth of experience and expertise, and knows their local packrafting patch well, is by far the best way to form a solid foundation on which to build longer, wilder, more self-sufficient adventures. Many also offer equipment hire, so you can give packrafting a go before committing to buying your own kit. You'll find a list of accredited guides who operate in the areas suggested here in the Resources section of this book.

Some of the best packrafting and bikerafting destinations are those with bodies of inland water that aren't reachable by car. Flat water, such as lakes and lochs, is easier and safer for beginners to paddle, particularly if your raft is heavily laden with

Scotland

Scotland's remote north-west coast could have been made specifically for packrafting. The peninsula of Knoydart, inaccessible by car and dotted with lochs and lochans; Inverpolly, an area of Wester Ross, which is as much water as land; serene Loch Maree, whose 13-mile (21.7km) length is scattered with more than 40 islands; and Scotland's beautiful, fast-flowing rivers, some of which can be rafted from source to sea.

Alaska

Alaska's vast reaches of untouched wilderness are a dream for packrafting. Wrangell-St. Elias National Park & Preserve is a landscape of jagged peaks, lakes and rivers with a great variety of packrafting potential.

New Zealand

Fiordland National Park on New Zealand's South Island is another stellar packrafting destination. From day trips on the Waiau River to longer expeditions, trekking through the park's rugged wilderness, paddling across alpine lakes and camping on tiny, uninhabited islands, there's infinite adventure potential.

Stand-up paddleboard (SUP) camping

SUPs are popular and convenient, inflating quickly and easily to provide a stable platform for exploring, swimming or relaxing that simply deflates and packs away after use. Camping with your SUP can be a delightful way to spend a sunny summer weekend.

There's not a lot of space for kit on a SUP but, unless you have a support team to carry your kit for you, adventures are anyway also limited to good weather and short journeys compared with other methods of travel, so you won't need to take much.

What to take

Go as minimalist as you're happy with, and pack everything in a waterproof bag that you can attach to the deck without exceeding the board's weight limit or upsetting the balance. As this is most likely to be a summer-only adventure, you'll only need a lightweight sleeping bag, while the board itself makes a good sleeping mat so you don't need to pack an extra one. A tarp to pitch over the top using your paddle as

a support offers shelter and privacy. Use the stuff sack from your sleeping bag to create an attachment point between the tarp and paddle by placing it over one end of the paddle and using the drawcord or other fastening on the bag as a tie point.

The ability to carry water is limited on a SUP. A water bag or hydration bladder, fixed securely to the board, works better than bottles. If you're paddling on a freshwater river or lake, a good-quality

▶ Exploring from the tent while the Kelly Kettle boils, River Usk

[251]

water filter is a lightweight and portable way to source safe drinking water. At the least, take a small, lightweight camping stove with sufficient gas, a mug, pan, spoon and reliable source of ignition, along with the food you'll need for the duration of the trip – or research places you'll be able to buy food en route. Even in summer, coastal areas can be cool and breezy in the mornings and evenings, so packing a lightweight insulated jacket is a good idea.

▲ SUP camping adventures in the French Alps

Where to go

Because of the lack of storage space, SUP camping is more limited than other boat-based adventures. But there's a lot of joy to be found in its simplicity, and it's a great choice for summertime one- or two-night breaks when you know the weather's going to be kind. An afternoon paddle along a lake or river, followed by a beach camp and then a relaxed return journey the next morning is a great adventure. If you paddle upstream or against the current on the way out, you can be reasonably sure that the return journey will be easier the next day. Because of their lack of manoeuvrability compared with canoes and kayaks, flat water is best for SUP adventures.

Small island groups work well for water-based camping adventures, particularly in places like Scotland that combine intricate coastlines with legal wild camping. Always be aware of tides and currents, pitch well clear of the water, and take care not to damage or disturb local flora and fauna.

Many places close to lakes, lochs, rivers and the coast also have campsites, offering an easy stop-over with facilities and water, particularly in busier areas.

TOP TIP

CHOOSING YOUR ADVENTURE

1 Camping can be the primary reason for going on a trip, or it can be a convenient, portable, affordable accommodation option. If there's something you've always wanted to do, or somewhere you've always wanted to go, why not plan a camping trip around it?

2 Camping is perfect for longer adventures as it doesn't tie you to a particular place and you can carry everything you need with you. Follow a long-distance trail on foot, bike or vehicle; explore a river or shoreline in a canoe or kayak. Either start by thinking about the adventure you'd like to go on and then plan the kit you need to do it, or, if you've already got plenty of kit, think about the most amazing adventures you could do with it.

▼ Canoe camping adventure with Wilderness Scotland

Photography

Leave nothing but footprints, take nothing but photos … but how do you take a great camping picture? Here are our tips:

- Choose your place wisely. So many beautiful locations have become Instagram clichés, so how can you create something different? Try a new angle on a classic or jog a mile from the crowds and you'll probably find you have the place to yourself.
- Pick the best light. Taking photos in good light makes the colours 'pop' and brings depth and richness to your images. Use the magical first light of early mornings and the minutes before sunset to capture the camping experience. Head out in spring and autumn when the slanting sun illuminates the colours, rather than midsummer when it washes them out.
- Think about the composition and tidy up any random shoes, food or rubbish that's in the frame. Check over every part of the image and make sure it's all just as you want it.
- Look for an image that tells a story about the place or trip. Friends and camping companions doing something in shot can bring the picture to life: adjusting a guy line, having a drink, tending the fire or similar will create a

more interesting, engaging photo than if they're simply sitting or standing about. Experiment with what works for you and have the camera ready: sometimes the best pictures aren't planned at all.

- If you want to be a bit more structured and planned with your photos, a tripod is a useful tool, allowing longer-exposure night-time shots, or enabling you to set up a photo, use the self-timer and appear in it yourself.
- If you have a camera with lens options, a wide-angle lens is great for capturing the tent in the landscape.
- Learning how to use photo editing software is a useful skill that means you can crop, edit and bring your images to life even if your original shot wasn't the perfect one you hoped for.

▲ Check your shots regularly to make sure you're happy with the composition and light

▶ Sunset and sunrise always make for a good photo

The glowing tent

One of the classic camping shots shows a glowing tent nestled beneath a spectacular starry sky. To create the glowing tent, you need to place a lantern or torch inside. Torches on a lower power setting often work well and sometimes more than one light will give a more even light distribution. Watch out for items that cause strange shadows or pinpoints of light. Many cameras and phones will have an automatic night mode, so have a go with this and you may be able to take a brilliant photo. If your camera has manual controls then go full manual; otherwise, if you start with the following settings and adjust them to suit the specific conditions, you should be able to get a great night-time image.

Tripod: You need to have the camera in a steady position. A tripod works best but you can also balance the camera on a cushion or jacket. Set the camera to take an image with the self-timer so you don't end up with camera shake from you pressing the button. You can also get in the image if you'd like to but remember to keep still or you will be blurry.

Shutter speed: The longer the shutter is open, the more light the camera will capture and the brighter the image. Start with something between 5 and 30 seconds and then experiment.

ISO: This is how sensitive the camera is to light. A higher ISO makes a brighter image but if it's too high the image will be grainy and lack definition. Start somewhere between 800 and 3,200. The best cameras and lenses will be able to go higher but a compact may be best set between 800 and 1,600.

Aperture: This is the hole in the lens that allows the light in. A wider aperture will let in more light, which is what you need for night-time photography. Set the camera to the lowest f number possible.

Focus: Turn the focus to infinity so as to capture both the stars and the glowing tent. Check your images and if they are a bit blurry you may need to adjust the focus slightly.

Bird's-eye view

If you have a drone and you are in an area that allows you to fly it, you can get a different perspective of your tent that can look great. This works best if you have a brightly coloured tent, because the tent will pop in the landscape and draw the eye to it. Of course, it also looks best if you can pitch somewhere amazing, like on a mountain, by a lake or on a beach.

06

Caring and repairing

Outdoor kit doesn't come cheap. Much of it is also made using plastics that will continue to exist long after we, as individuals, have struck our last camp. So it makes good sense to spend time researching and considering what to buy – something that we hope this book will go some way towards helping with – and then looking after that kit so it has a long and productive life.

The art of caring and repairing is seeing a resurgence at the moment, fuelled by the climate crisis and cost of living crisis combined. Brilliantly, this means resources abound on how to patch, darn, sew and glue just about anything, with thoughtfully made blogs and videos widely available online. The number of repair cafes and outdoor shops and brands that offer repair services is also growing all the time – a much-needed counter to the thoughtless, wasteful and exploitative fast fashion industry.

Back in the days when we worked in an outdoor shop, we fixed and replaced a lot of broken tents and replaced broken poles and pegs for campers who'd underestimated Devon's moorland and coastal weather. Sometimes they'd just been unlucky: the weather was worse than expected or someone tripped over a guy line or the entrance to the tent. Ultimately though, in most cases, if the tent had been pitched correctly, using all the guy lines and peg points, thinking about the wind direction, and making sure the tent flaps were properly closed, the damage would have been avoided or reduced. Another common complaint was damage caused by putting the tent away damp and then leaving it until

▲ Sponging the tent down before drying it out and packing it away ready for the next adventure

the next camping trip a year later. It was a good lesson for us to learn, too, and we now always take time to properly dry out and air our tent and other kit before storing it away so it can continue to perform well for many years.

Camping kit is fairly expensive, but it will last a long time and be a pleasure to use if it is looked after well. We'll move on to repairs later in this chapter, but preventing damage happening in the first place is much easier than repairing it, so here are our top tips for keeping your kit in good nick:

- Check the weather forecast shortly before you leave and throughout your trip to make sure your set-up is likely to be able to withstand the conditions.
- Think about wind direction and pitch your tent with a streamlined profile to the wind.
- Check the ground before you pitch to prevent sharp rocks or sticks puncturing the groundsheet.
- Always use all the guy lines and pegging points to give your tent the best chance of standing up to bad weather.
- Secure the tent flaps in a closed position to stop the wind entering. If a strong wind is able to get in and fill a tent, even the best mountain tent can rip or blow away.
- If you notice pole sections starting to fail, replace them or splint them immediately. If they snap, they can tear the fabric (see advice on repairing poles later in this chapter).
- Check everything carefully as you're putting it away at the end of a trip and make a note of any issues so that you can sort them before the next trip.
- Re-waterproof your tent every couple of years or when water droplets that land on the fabric stop beading up and rolling off (see how to reproof your tent later in this chapter).
- Open everything out at home within a couple of days of your return, and make sure it's all clean and dry before you put it away.
- Store camping kit in a dark and dry place.

Cleaning kit

If you need to clean the tent after use, it's easiest to pitch it and wash the flysheet using a soft sponge and water. Specialist tent cleaning liquids are available from brands like Nikwax and Grangers, which are formulated to clean without damaging the fabric or reducing its ability to shed water. You can use a garden hose to gently rinse off any dust, dirt or remaining soap but don't use high-pressure water.

The groundsheet is likely to get dirty after use, especially if it's been wet while you've been camping. To clean the groundsheet, lay it out on the ground, fold it in half and wash the exposed half using a sponge and water: a suitable cleaning liquid can help if it's particularly muddy. Leave that side to dry thoroughly and then fold it the other way around and wash the other side.

Once clean, leave the tent pitched to make sure it's completely dry before you pack it away.

Zips can start to stick if they get contaminated with dust and grit. Open the zip and give it a wipe with a damp cloth. There are also special zip cleaners and lubricants available. Close the zip again and feel if it's smoother; running the zip open and closed a few times will often help. Make sure metal zips are dry before storing for any length of time.

▶ Applying Gear Aid zipper lubricant to help keep the zipper running smoothly

Repairing kit

Being able to fix your kit while away can save a camping trip. Achieving a first-aid-style repair to keep everything functioning until you planned to get home is the first aim; you can repair properly or replace later. We always carry a repair kit with us, but its contents will vary with the type of camping and the equipment we have with us. In all cases, I want to be able to fix a tent pole, replace a guy line, repair a puncture in a sleeping mat, fix the strap on a rucksack or sew together a hole in some clothing or equipment. This is what we carry when car camping or backpacking:

◀ Repairing a small rip using a Tenacious Tape patch

WATERPROOFING KIT

A NEW NYLON, polyester or polycotton tent will arrive with a water-repellent treatment applied to the flysheet. This makes water bead up and roll off the fabric rather than allowing the rain to soak into it. Over time and use, this treatment will wear off and you need to replace or reproof it to keep your tent as waterproof as possible. It's normally recommended that you reproof your tent every couple of years, but this obviously depends on use. The tent will need reproofing when water starts to soak into the flysheet rather than beading up and running off. You can buy reproofing solutions designed specifically for the fabric of your tent from all good outdoor shops. We recommend Nikwax or Grangers, both of whom produce environmentally friendly water-based and PFC-free cleaning and reproofing solutions. Follow the instructions on the bottle, which will normally be something like this:

- Pitch the tent and make sure it's clean by giving it a gentle rinse with a hose or sponge down, using a tent cleaning product if necessary. Reproofing agents work best on a slightly damp fabric.

- Spray on the reproofer and wipe using a damp cloth or sponge to cover all the flysheet.
- Leave for a couple of minutes, then rinse the tent with a clean damp cloth.
- Dry fully before packing away.

The seams of the flysheet are normally taped or sealed to prevent water leaking through the gap between fabrics or the stitch holes. Over time, the tape can come off or you might notice a new leak along a seam. Either way, the simple solution is to reseal the seam. Several companies make a seam sealer; we like Gear Aid. Make sure you get the right product for the fabric of your tent. Seam sealers normally contain some nasty solvents so always do this outside:

- Spread the flysheet of the tent out on a flat, dry surface with the inside facing up. Sometimes it's easiest to pitch the tent with the flysheet inside out.
- Make sure the seams are clean and dry. You may need to give them a wash or spend some time removing the old seam tape.
- Follow the manufacturer's instructions – normally to brush a thin coating of the seam sealer all along the seam.
- Wipe off any excess sealer with a damp cloth.
- Leave to dry for at least as long as recommended, otherwise your tent may stick together when you pack it away.

- pole sleeve
- duct tape
- strong nylon cord
- puncture repair kit
- zip ties
- strong string
- needle and thimble
- Swiss army knife or multi-tool
- Tenacious Tape

If we're racing or trying to be as light as possible, we may not carry everything, but this could mean we can't finish the race due to broken kit, or the experience is a lot less fun. The few extra grams in the repair kit could save the day.

▲ Tenacious Tape patches, also available in standard shapes or as a roll to cut

KIT FIRST AID TIPS

THESE ARE DESIGNED to be quick fixes using the tools and materials you are likely to have with you on a trip. The repairs should get you to the end of the trip but you need to revisit them at home before you take the kit out on the next adventure.

To fix a **snapped pole**, remove the pole from the tent and thread a pole sleeve over the broken section and, if possible, tape it in place. If you don't have a pole sleeve you can use a couple of tent pegs or any other strong and thin items to splint the pole at the break. Then continue to use the pole as normal.

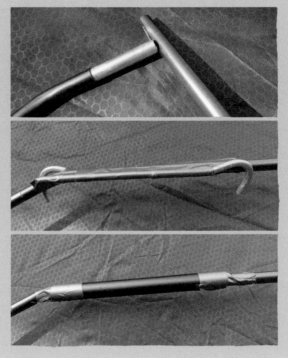

▶ *Top*: A snapped aluminium tent pole
Middle: Splinted with a tent peg
Bottom: Splinted with a pole sleeve

Home repairs

The following repairs will take a bit longer and some require a sewing machine or spare parts that you're unlikely to have ready to go. The outcome should be that whatever you're repairing is fixed and ready for the next adventure. It might even look better with a cool visible mend and it's certainly going to add to your sense of accomplishment. There are lots of online resources with step-by-step and video instructions available. Some of the best are referenced at the back of this book.

Poles

If you have a broken tent pole, you can normally replace the section of pole that's damaged. Contact the shop that you bought the tent from or the manufacturer to get a new pole section of the correct length and diameter. To replace it, pull the end out of the pole and untie the elastic cord, remove the broken section of pole and replace it with the new one, thread the pole sections back on to the cord and tie it back into the end cap. It's easiest to do this with the pole fitted together rather than folded as the elastic will be under less tension.

The elastic cord that joins the poles together will lose its stretch over time,

Snapped guy lines or peg attachment loops can be replaced with strong cord. Don't worry about reattaching the tensioning systems, just cut the cord to the specific length you need.

Broken zips can sometimes be repaired simply by rethreading the zip puller and being careful to straighten out any bent teeth. If this doesn't work, you can sew a zip closed and put up with just one entrance or a smaller opening until the end of the trip.

Rips in a tent's flysheet can be roughly sewn together and then taped over to add strength and weatherproof-ness. If the tear is in an area that will be stretched tightly or if the weather is bad, sewing a patch of other material over the tear can add strength to the repair. If you don't have any repair patches, scavenge the material from non-critical clothing or equipment.

Straps can be sewn if you have a strong needle and a thimble or something to help you push the needle through tough

materials. Often, you can simply tie the remaining strap on to some new strap or cord and use it like that.

Broken buckles can be replaced by borrowing a buckle from a less important strap. Alternatively, you can use a zip tie to keep a buckle closed or remove the buckle and tie the straps.

Most **air-filled sleeping pads** will come with a puncture repair kit and instructions. In general, these are like fixing a bike's inner tube. Clean and dry the area around the puncture, then apply the glue or patch. Patches with rounded edges are less likely to peel off so trim a square patch to remove the corners. Press it down and hold it flat until it's stuck. Leave to dry and then use as normal.

A puncture in an inflatable pole used in air-beam-style tents can be repaired with a patch in the same way as an air-filled bed. Most tents will come with a puncture repair kit and instructions.

going saggy and not helping when you try to pitch the tent. You can buy new elastic cord from most camping shops. You need unstretched elastic the length of the pole minus one pole section. To replace the cord, pull out the end cap and cut or untie the old elastic. Remove the elastic, keeping the pole sections in the correct order. Tie the new elastic to one end cap then thread the pole sections back on to the elastic. You will have to stretch the elastic to allow you to add the last couple of pole sections and tie the end into the end cap.

Patching

It's best to use a sewing machine to patch items because it's hard to stitch as accurately and strongly by hand. Saying that, it is possible and sometimes there's just no way to get to a rip in a larger item with a sewing machine. To patch a rip or hole in fabric, work out the size of the patch needed to cover the area then add about 1cm (⅜in) all around to allow for a seam. Cut the patch out, turn in the seams and iron flat to make it easier to sew. Line up the patch exactly where you need it and pin it on to the item to make it easier to sew.

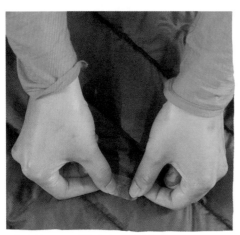

▲ Patching a small hole in a sleeping bag

Use a top stitch to sew through both layers of patch fabric and the repaired item, sew all the way around and lock off the ends by sewing forwards and backwards a few times. Turn the repair over and either patch the inside as well, sew the rip closed or cut the repaired fabric away from the patch; the object of this is to stop the tear catching and ripping again. If the item that you've patched is waterproof, you need to seal the seams (see page 263).

A stick-on patch is easy to use at home or when out on an adventure. They are good for repairing waterproof fabrics and don't need seam sealing. To use, follow the instructions of the specific patch for the specific fabric. In general, make sure that the fabric you are patching is clean and totally dry. Trim the patch to remove any sharp corners that are likely to peel away. Stick the patch on, apply pressure to help it seal and allow it to dry. Then you should be good to go.

Zips

Zips can stick, the puller can snap, or the puller can come off the end of the zip. Happily, these are all repairable.

- A sticky zip first needs a clean in some water to remove any grit or debris. Once dry, apply a tiny amount of oil to a metal zip or rub a pencil on the teeth of a plastic zip; the graphite from the pencil will act as a lubricant. Silicone spray will also work with a plastic grip but try to use as little as possible. When this is done, run the zip all the way backwards and forwards a few times until it feels smooth.
- A broken puller can make opening or closing a zip much harder. Hopefully the zip still has the metal loop on the

Darning

DARNING PROVED REALLY HANDY recently when our awesome spaniel decided to lovingly chew my favourite woolly hat.

Darning is actually really simple; you can use it to fix small holes in woolly or fleecy fabrics. Choose a matching colour thread to make a near invisible mend or a contrasting colour for a trendy visible mend. Start from the inside of the fabric and sew stiches across the hole in one direction. Then sew at 90 degrees to the first set of stiches, weaving the new stiches through the first set. Continue this until you have completely covered the hole. Lock off the end of the thread by sewing several stiches in the same place and then cut off the ends.

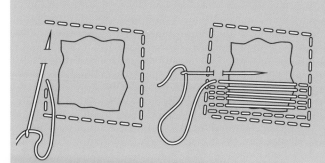

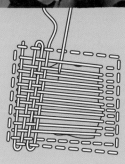

puller, and you can attach a small loop of cord to act as a puller. If the loop has snapped, you will need to replace the puller (see below).

- A damaged zip puller that doesn't close the zip properly can be replaced. Contact the manufacturer via the shop from which you bought the product to get the correct replacement zip.
- For open zips (like a jacket where the two halves of the zip come apart completely), use pliers or wire cutters to open the zip stop at the top of the zip, slide the old puller off and slide the new one on. Reattach the zip stop, using

pliers to squeeze it closed.

- For closed zips (like a jacket pocket or a tent inner flap) you will need to pick out the stiches at the bottom of the zip so that you can slide off the damaged puller. Slide on the new puller to both sets of teeth so that it closes the zip. Sew the end of the zip back together so that the slider can't fall off the end.

Buckles

Broken buckles can be replaced at home and don't normally need sewing. Buckles are sized by the width of the webbing they fit on to. You can buy new buckles from most outdoor companies – sometimes they will send you some for free. It's best to ask the shop from which you bought the product first, since they may have a buckle, or they can contact the manufacturer for you. Otherwise, contact the manufacturer directly. You can also buy the generic buckles in a range of sizes, but this will mean that you will probably have to replace both the male and female side. Buckles will either be threaded on or sewn on to the straps. Threaded buckles are easy – simply rethread the new buckle. To replace a sewn buckle there are three options:

1   Unpick the stiches, rethread the new buckle and sew it back together.
2   Unpick the stiches, thread on the new buckle and add a ladder lock buckle to secure the strap without sewing.
3   Cut the broken buckle off without unstitching the webbing. Use a new buckle with a removable or open release pin so that you can thread it on to the sewn loop.

Professional repairs

Sometimes repairs need to be done by a professional. Many outdoor companies offer an inhouse repair service for their own products regardless of the age and amount of use, so we'd suggest contacting them first. If they can't help, there are several companies who specialise in outdoor kit repair who probably can. In most cases, it will be cheaper and nicer to repair rather than replace. Look for local shoe repair shops, which will have very strong sewing machines and may be able to stich rucksack webbing as well as shoes. A local caravan awning or marquee company may also be able to help with repairs to heavy fabrics that are difficult to sew by hand.

Storage

All of your fabric camping gear is best stored somewhere cool, dark and free from damp. Tents are fine stored in their storage bags as long as they are completely dry when you put them away. Sleeping bags should be stored uncompressed to maintain the ability of the filling to loft. Most sleeping bags come with a large storage sack for this, but you can use a big pillowcase if not. Self-inflating or air-filled sleep pads are best stored unrolled with the valve open to allow any moisture to escape; ours live unrolled under the bed.

> **TOP TIP**
>
> ### LOOKING AFTER YOUR CAMPING KIT
>
> 1   Clean and inspect your kit when you get back from a trip. Sort any repairs or replacements then rather than in a rush when you're packing for the next trip. Always store kit clean and dry.
>
> 2   Repairs are often achievable with a basic sewing kit, tape and glue. There are lots of how-to videos and instructions online. If it's beyond you, contact the shop from which you bought the item, the manufacturer or a professional repair company.
>
> 3   Carry a simple repair kit on camping trips and adventures. A quick repair may allow you to continue the trip rather than having to head home, where you can get it fixed or do it properly yourself.

USEFUL KNOTS

IF YOU KNOW HOW to tie a few knots then you can probably deal with most situations. We think these are most useful for camping:

Fisherman's knot – Very useful for repairing snapped guy lines, this knot joins two ropes or cords together and it doesn't matter if they are different thicknesses.

Tent hitch or taut-line knot – An adjustable loop knot that is useful for attaching guy lines as it's easy to make the loop larger or smaller.

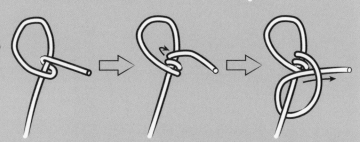

Clove hitch – This is a quick knot that can be used to tie a rope to a stake. It's also useful when improvising a shelter with some waterproof fabric.

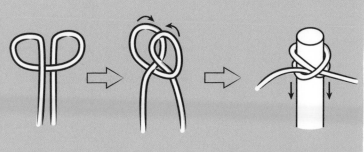

 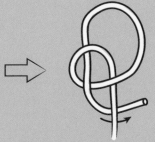 

Bowline – A strong knot used to tie something to something else. This can be used to tie a rope around a tree or through a closed ring or eyelet.

Kit lists

Car camping

Overview

The primary aim of a car camping set-up is an enjoyable experience and comfortable sleep. Space and weight are far less of an issue than they are when you're backpacking, although families may wish to consider adding a roof box or small trailer as it's amazing how much you can end up trying to fit in one car.

☑ **Shelter** – Tents suitable for car camping trips include tunnel, dome, pod and bell tents with poles or air beams. They need to be large enough for everyone, with head room to stand up in and separate bedrooms if necessary. A windbreak and/or tarp/canopy can provide additional weather protection, privacy and a dry outside space.

☑ **Sleeping on** – Airbeds and self-inflating mats, possibly with a foam mat underneath for extra insulation, and frame-based camp cots all offer warm and comfortable sleeping options. Size and weight are secondary although still important.

☑ **Sleeping in** – Sleeping bags need to be warm enough for the expected night-time temperature but can be square for extra foot room as size and weight are no issue. Sleeping bag liners add warmth, comfort and washability. Duvets and blankets are perfectly acceptable, and often more comfortable. A couple of extra blankets are a good idea as an additional warm layer. Proper pillows.

☑ **Cooking and eating** – Stable and practical double- or single-burner gas stoves, canister gas stoves, barbecue, pizza oven, fire pit. Pans, frying pan, steamer, utensils, mugs, plates, bowls and cutlery, which can be camping specific or from home. Washing-up bowl, sponge and liquid.

☑ **Power and lighting** – If you're using electric hook-up at a campsite you'll need a suitable cable to connect to the site supply. Chargers for phones, laptops etc. Lighting can be plug-in or gas/battery/chargeable electric. If no hook-up is available, charging and power from a vehicle is an option or a solar power and battery set-up.

☑ **Extras** – Camping chairs and table, cushions, toys/games, guidebooks, maps, first aid kit.

Backpacking

Overview

Everything for the duration of your trip, other than food and water, needs to fit in a rucksack that's still comfortable enough to carry for many miles of walking. Low weight and pack size is therefore important, but unlike ultralight backpacking set-ups there's still room for a few extras to keep things comfortable.

☑ **Shelter** – Tents suitable for backpacking can be tunnel, semi- or fully geodesic dome, or single pole design, depending on the amount of internal space you prefer. In general, match your tent to the number of people sleeping in it; however, a lone hiker may choose a small, two-person tent for longer trips, especially in poor weather, to allow for more room inside. Go for low height (so you can't stand up) to improve weather resistance and reduce weight. A light tarp can be used to extend the porch.

☑ **Sleeping on** – Foam mats, self-inflating mats or lightweight air pads. Possibly ultra-light camp cots. Weight and pack size are important factors.

☑ **Sleeping in** – Sleeping bags or quilts suitable for the likely night-time temperatures. Consider a sleeping bag liner to add warmth, comfort and washability.

☑ **Cooking and eating** – Gas canister stoves or liquid fuel burners. Lightweight pan set plus a mug and bowl. Minimal utensils and cutlery.

☑ **Power and lighting** – Portable solar charging or rechargeable power packs are useful for keeping phones and other devices charged. Lightweight battery/USB-chargeable lanterns or head torches.

☑ **Extras** – Ultra-light chair/stool. Guidebook, maps and other navigation equipment, cards, first aid kit, repair kit.

Ultra-light camping

Overview

When you're fast-and-light hiking, running or fastpacking (a mixture of the two), low weight and small pack size are key. You won't get the same comfort or convenience that you would if you were moving slower with a larger pack, but you'll be able to cover the ground far more quickly and easily.

✓ **Shelter** – Ultra-light tent, bivi bag or tarp suitable for the conditions and number of people to reduce weight. Weight and pack size are more important than comfort so be prepared to compromise on space inside the tent. In warm, dry conditions, a shelter may not be needed.

✓ **Sleeping on** – Ultra-light air pad or foam mat. Some superlight campers even use bubble wrap or simply the foam padding from the back of a pack along with other clothing, a rope etc to add insulation from the ground. Weight is more important than comfort to a point, although the ability to get good sleep is of course still important.

✓ **Sleeping in** – Lightweight, packable sleeping bag or quilt. Down is often lightest. Wear clothes, such as a full set of Merino wool base layers, to reduce the required temperature rating (and therefore the weight) of the sleeping bag.

✓ **Cooking and eating** – Lightweight gas canister stove or liquid fuel burner. You could also consider an ultra-light wood burning stove so that you don't need to carry fuel. Choose a pan that doubles as a mug, and combined cutlery such as a Spork or Tifoon.

✓ **Power and lighting** – Rechargeable power pack, phone charger. Head torches (main + spare).

✓ **Extras** – Maps and other navigation equipment. First aid kit. Repair kit.

Bikepacking and cycle touring

Overview

Packsize is all important for bikepacking and cycle touring, as everything needs to fit into a set of small bags, but weight isn't as crucial as when you're on foot. In wet conditions, bikes kick up a lot of spray as they go, so it's essential your kit is waterproof from every angle.

✓ **Shelter** – Ultra-light tent, bivi bag or tarp suitable for the conditions and number of people to reduce weight. Weight and pack size are more important than comfort so be prepared to compromise on space inside the tent. In warm, dry conditions, a shelter may not be needed.

✓ **Sleeping on** – Ultra-light air pad or foam mat.

✓ **Sleeping in** – Lightweight, packable sleeping bag or quilt. Down is often lightest. Wear clothes, such as a full set of Merino wool base layers, to reduce the required temperature rating (and therefore the weight) of the sleeping bag.

✓ **Cooking and eating** – Lightweight gas canister stove or liquid fuel burner. Choose a pan that doubles as a mug, and combined cutlery such as a Spork or Tifoon.

✓ **Power and lighting** – Rechargeable power pack, phone charger. Head torch and bike lights plus spare/rechargeable batteries.

✓ **Extras** – Maps and other navigation equipment. First aid kit. Repair kit. Basic bike tools, spare innertube, pump, bike lock and bike lights. A pair of light flip-flops are a nice change from cleated bike shoes and can be easily strapped on to the outside of a bike bag.

◄ Reliable waterproofing with Ortlieb cycle panniers

Mountains and other exposed/weather-affected areas

Overview

Depending on the specifics of your adventure, you may be carrying this set-up on foot or travelling by bike, canoe or vehicle, so space and weight could be important but the priority is kit that copes with the expected weather. Be prepared to accept some extra weight in order to provide the strength, durability and warmth demanded by the conditions.

☑ **Shelter** – Tents should be strong geodesic or semi-geodesic style; some of the more robust tunnel designs are also suitable. Take extra care to choose the correct pegs or ground anchors, especially if pitching on rock or snow. Weight is slightly less important than robustness and weather resistance.

☑ **Sleeping on** – If you're going to be sleeping on cold ground, extra insulation is essential. A foam mat underneath a self-inflating or light air-pad-style mat adds insulation for very little weight or expense.

☑ **Sleeping in** – Sleeping bags must have good warmth for the weight and can be a high fill-power down or synthetic. Sleeping in warm clothing is also important

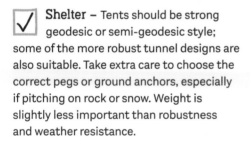

for maintaining heat overnight. A vapour barrier sleeping bag liner may be used to maintain loft in a down bag.

☑ **Cooking and eating** – Canister gas stoves with a winter gas mix or liquid multi-fuel stoves. Bear in mind that extra fuel may be required to melt snow for water. Gas type is important at high altitude or lower temperatures. Pan, mug, spoon.

☑ **Power and lighting** – Portable solar charging. Light battery/USB-chargeable lanterns and head torches.

☑ **Extras** – Potential for extended time in the tent due to poor weather so consider entertainment such as cards, books etc. Personal protective equipment as required. Navigation equipment, first aid kit, spares and repair kit.

Canoe and kayak camping

Overview

In a canoe or kayak, space is often more limited than weight as the weight of the boat is supported by the water. Bear in mind that heavy boats may need to be unloaded for portaging (carrying). The boat and paddle can often be used as part of your shelter. Everything should be stowed securely and packed in waterproof bags.

☑ **Shelter** – A tent, tarp or bivi bag suitable for the weather conditions and surfaces you're likely to be pitching on. The canoe and paddles can be used to help pitch a tarp, which may mean you don't need to take poles. Free-standing tents are easier to pitch on beaches or rocky islands than tunnel designs, so may be the best choice for kayak adventures. In a sea kayak the size of the hatches may dictate the maximum size of any one item.

☑ **Sleeping on** – Self-inflating air mats offer the best combination of packable comfort and insulation.

☑ **Sleeping in** – Sleeping bags should be suitable for the expected temperatures. Synthetic fill is normally better because it doesn't matter as much if it gets wet but synthetic tends to be bulkier than down. Well worth double-bagging sleeping kit just in case.

☑ **Cooking and eating** – Canister gas, liquid fuel or solid fuel burning stoves. Wood is often available on beaches and shorelines so lightweight box stoves or storm kettles can be used effectively. Cooking pot, cutlery, bowl, mug.

☑ **Power and lighting** – Portable solar charging can work well in calm weather. LED lanterns, rechargeable head torches and power banks can be carried.

☑ **Extras** – Personal protective and safety kit including buoyancy aid, first aid kit, whistle and knife. Spares and repair kit for the kayak/canoe and paddle. Water filter and/or water bottles/bags to carry water for the day. Spare waterproof/dry bags. Large, lightweight, packable bags (such as the big blue ones from Ikea) are invaluable for transporting everything from boat to camp and back again.

Resources

Online

Camping and campsites

- Campsite finding and booking at Hip Camp: www.hipcamp.com
- For UK and European campsite bookings, lots of camping information and the benefits of club membership: www.campingandcaravanningclub.co.uk
- For campsites, food recommendations and wild attractions in the UK and beyond, check the local Wild Guide: www.wildthingspublishing.com

Caring and repairing

- Repair guides to help you fix outdoor clothing and equipment with videos and step-by-step instructions, by Vaude but not brand specific: help.vaude.com/care-repair
- Repair products such as seam grip and patches as well as instructions for caring and repairing outdoor clothing and equipment: www.gearaid.com
- Environmentally friendly waterproofing and cleaning products and instructions to find out how to wash and reproof different types of fabric and equipment by Nikwax: www.nikwax.com or Grangers: www.grangers.co.uk

Outdoor cooking

- Bushcraft and camp kitchen products including the Andy Handy from the Ray Mears store: www.raymears.com/Bushcraft_Products
- Recycle used gas canisters with a Jetboil CrunchIt: www.jetboil.com

Outdoor living, safety and survival skills and equipment

- Leave No Trace information and resources for responsible camping: www.lnt.org
- Recreate Responsibly, a guide to camping sustainably: www.recreateresponsibly.org
- Outdoor skills, equipment and training information, and adventure travel insurance (UK): www.thebmc.co.uk

- Equipment, skills, travel inspiration and information: www.msrgear.com/blog
- Gear, routes and inspirational articles from UK outdoor magazines Trail and Country Walking: www.livefortheoutdoors.com
- Equipment information, gear rental and Rab jacket and sleeping bag servicing (UK): www.rab.equipment/uk
- Outdoor access, skills, routes, gear and travel by the Ramblers: www.ramblers.org.uk
- Mosquito nets and insect repellent from Lifesystems: www.lifesystems.co.uk
- PMD-based natural insect repellents and information from Incognito: www.lessmosquito.com
- First aid step-by-step instructions, information, equipment, training (in the UK) and a free app that works offline and includes instructions for most first aid scenarios. St John Ambulance: www.sja.org.uk
- Bushcraft and wilderness survival information, teaching and expeditions with HowlBushcraft: www.howlbushcraft.com
- Bushcraft and wilderness skills, courses and events with Manse Ahmad and Wilderness Pioneers: www.wildernesspioneers.co.uk

- Guided adventure holidays in the Highlands and Islands of Scotland: www.wildernessscotland.com

Camping with bikes, canoes, kayaks, SUPs and rafts

- Bikepacking information and guides: www.bikepacking.com
- Canoes and information about canoe travel: www.oldtowncanoe.com
- Alpacka Raft purchasing and packrafting information: www.alpackaraft.com
- Bikerafting (packrafting with a bike): www.bikepacking.com/plan/bikerafting-guide
- Packrafting in Scotland: www.backcountry.scot/packraftingtrips
- The American Packrafting Association: www.packraft.org
- Packrafting New Zealand: www.packraftingnz.com

Great outdoor brands for high quality, responsibly made kit:

- Alpkit clothing and equipment: www.alpkit.com
- BioLite solar panels, lighting and stoves: https://uk.bioliteenergy.com/
- Esbit stoves and accessories: www.esbit.de/en
- Fjällräven clothing and equipment: www.fjallraven.com/uk
- Helinox camp furniture: www.helinox.eu
- Hilleberg strong and lightweight tents: www.hilleberg.com/eng
- Isbjörn children's outdoor clothing: www.isbjornofsweden.com/en
- Kelly Kettle cooking kit: www.kellykettle.com
- Klättermusen outdoor clothing: www.klattermusen.com/en
- MSR stoves and outdoor equipment: www.msrgear.com/ie
- Opinel knives: www.opinel.com/en
- Ortlieb bikepacking and cycle touring bags: www.ortlieb.com/uk_en
- Petromax outdoor cooking equipment: www.petromax.com
- Primus lightweight stoves and cooking equipment: www.primusequipment.com/en-eu
- Sierra Designs clothing and equipment: www.sierradesigns.com
- Snow Peak stoves and cooking equipment: https://uk.snowpeak.com/
- Terra Nova tough, lightweight tents: www.terra-nova.co.uk
- Ticket to the Moon hammocks: www.ticketothemoon.com
- Thule roof tents, boxes and bike racks: www.thule.com/en-gb
- Trangia alcohol stoves: www.trangia.se/en
- Vaude outdoor clothing and equipment: www.vaude.com/be/en

Books

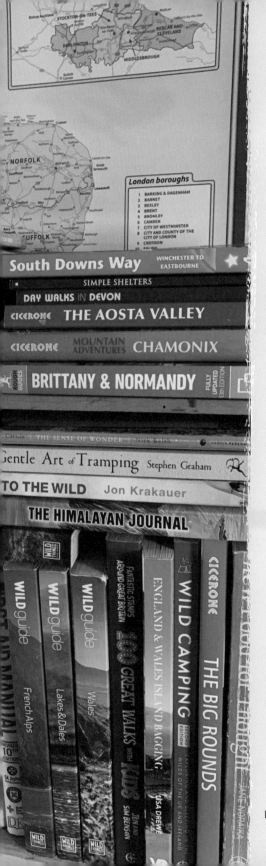

Benson, Jen and Sim, *The Adventurer's Guide to Britain*, Conway (2018)

Carr, Lizzie, *Paddling Britain*, Bradt Travel Guides (2018)

Donovan, Robin, *The Camp Dutch Oven Cookbook*, Rockridge Press (2017)

Goodwin, Ray, *Canoeing*, Pesda Press (2016)

Graham, Jenny, *Coffee First, Then the World*, Bloomsbury Sport (2023)

Hayes, Nick, *The Book of Trespass*, Bloomsbury (2021)

Hutchinson, Derek and Horodowich, Wayne, *The Complete Book of Sea Kayaking*, Falcon Guides (2018)

LeRoutard France camping guides, Hachette

Lonely Planet Under the Stars Europe, Lonely Planet (2022)

McJannet, Laurence, *Bikepacking*, Wild Things Publishing Ltd (2016)

Mears, Ray, *Wilderness Chef*, Conway (2020)

Moseley, Jo, *Stand-Up Paddleboarding in Great Britain*, Vertebrate Publishing Ltd (2022)

Neale, Stephen, *Wild Camping*, Conway (2020)

The instructional series of books by Mountain Training (UK): *Hillwalking, Navigation in the Mountains, International Mountain Trekking & Winter Skills*

Turnbull, Ronald, *The Book of the Bivvy*, Cicerone Press (2021)

Wild Guide series, Wild Things Publishing Ltd

◄ Adventure guides and inspiration

Picture credits

All photos are copyright of the authors, with the exception of:

2023 Oase Outdoors ApS: 107
Adobe Stock: 22–3, 68, 78, 88, 92, 95, 100, 112–13, 147, 185, 210, 257, 178–9
Alpkit: 143 (Top)
Andy Earl/Black Diamond: 229
Bard Basber/MSR: 195
The Camping and Caravanning Club: 46, 66
Courtney Cooper/Sierra Designs: 4 (Top Left), 32,
Creative Commons/Arup Malakar: 256,
    /Jeff Moser: 26, /Kitty Terwolbeck: 27,
    /OakleyOriginals: 124
Dafydd Wyn Morgan/Dark Skies Camping: 8
Daniel Ahlgren Adventure Production/Thule Sweden AB: 54–5
Emily Sierra Taylor Photography/Sierra Designs: 31, 49
Esbit: 155
Gear Aid: 5 (Bottom Right), 89, 262 (Top & Bottom), 264 (Top), 266
Getty: 2–3, 15, 59, 60, 64–6, 73, 74–5, 77, 81, 86, 94, 97, 98, 99, 103, 104, 110, 123, 126–7, 142, 145, 152, 161, 169, 175, 183, 194, 211, 220, 221, 223, 224–5, 228, 244, 246, 258–9, 271
Gordan Taylor: 254
Karl & Moa Gräsmark/Tentipi: 108 (Bottom)

Lars Schneider/Schneider Outdoor Visions/ Ortlieb: 241, 274
Lina Flodins/Tentipi: 48
Lost Meadow Treepod at Wildish Cornwall: 69
Manse Ahmad/Wilderness Pioneers: 4 (Top Right), 130–1, 132
Max Seigal/Tenstile: 53
Nadir Kahn/OMM: 12, 236
Paul Besley: 120, 154
Pencelli Castle Campsite: 4 (Bottom Left), 67
Peter Amend/Sierra Designs: 38
Quencha tents by Decathlon: 45
Ray Mears: 133
Scott Rinckenberger/MSR: 144, 148, 158
Selk'bags: 85
Sierra Designs: 16
Solo Stove: 136
Terra Nova: 41, 56
Thor Tingey/Alpacka Raft: 5 (Top Right), 248, 249, 250
Tom Kahle/Tentsile: 52
Vango: 33, 44
Wilderness Scotland: 253 (Bottom)

All photographs depicting wild camping are for illustrative purposes only and do not constitute permission or recommendation

Acknowledgements

Our heartfelt thanks to everyone who's helped us bring this book together, in particular Liz Multon, Kate Beer, Sutchinda Thompson, Austin Taylor and the rest of the brilliant Bloomsbury team, plus illustrators Dave Saunders and Alister Savage.

Huge thanks to fellow adventurers the Taylor and McGrogan families, Manse Ahmad, Wilderness Scotland, Dafydd Wyn Morgan, Ray Mears, Paul Besley, Renee McGregor and Ewen Malloch.

Thanks to outdoor brands Nordisk, Biolite, Kelly Kettle, Petromax, Terra Nova, Alpkit, MSR, The Camping & Caravanning Club,

Sierra Designs, Thule, Esbit, Gear Aid, Tentipi, Ortlieb, Tentsile, OMM, Alpacka Raft, Vango, Outwell, Selk' Bags, Solo Stove, Isbjorn, Black Diamond, Primus, Ticket to the Moon and Trail Outdoor Leisure/Portofino Paddleboards, and campsites Wildish Cornwall, Pencelli Castle and Dark Skies Llandovery.

Finally, a big thank you to our families for their unwavering support, especially Lucy, Sam, H & O for help with photoshoots and everyone at Mill for the use of the field. And, as always, our love and thanks to E & H for being the very best adventure companions in life and under canvas.

Index